PRAISE FOR *THE MINDFUL MANIFESTO*

'The Mindful Manifesto helps us to "be" more and to "do" less. It's old wisdom backed by modern science, beautifully described.'

– Professor Richard Layard, Wellbeing Programme Director, London School of Economics

'The Mindful Manifesto is a wonderful overview of mindfulness meditation – comprehensive, honest and compassionate. This book helps make mindfulness accessible to all.'

– Sharon Salzberg, author of *Lovingkindness* and *Real Happiness*

'Wise, sensible and helpful for all forms of emotional disorders from depression to anxiety and addiction. This book on mindfulness is a great step towards finding peace of mind.'

– Sally Brampton, author of *Shoot the Damn Dog*

'The Mindful Manifesto *offers a fresh perspective on ancient wisdom. It is authentic, timely and hugely needed.*'

– Peter J. Conradi, author of *Going Buddhist* and *Iris Murdoch*'

This book is really important. Mindfulness is the way forwards for dealing with depression and anxiety, and for general wellbeing.'

– Ruby Wax, comedian

'Readable, fascinating and incredibly relevant in our dangerously disconnected, stressed-out age.'

– Lucia Cockcroft, yogaabode.com

'Every single person, from prime ministers and presidents to "ordinary men and women", would benefit from practising mindfulness and stillness in their lives. This wisdom has been known for thousands of years and now the science has at last caught up with it. This book makes the case admirably clearly.'

– Dr. Anthony Seldon, headmaster Wellington College and author of *Blair*, *Blair Unbound*, *Brown at 10* and *Trust*

THE MINDFUL
MANIFESTO

THE MINDFUL MANIFESTO

HOW DOING LESS AND NOTICING MORE CAN HELP US THRIVE IN A STRESSED-OUT WORLD

DR JONTY HEAVERSEDGE & ED HALLIWELL

www.themindfulmanifesto.com

HAY HOUSE

Australia • Canada • Hong Kong • India
South Africa • United Kingdom • United States

First published and distributed in the United Kingdom by:
Hay House UK Ltd, Astley House, 33 Notting Hill Gate, London W11 3JQ
Tel: +44 (0)20 3675 2450; Fax: +44 (0)20 3675 2451
www.hayhouse.co.uk

Published and distributed in the United States of America by:
Hay House, Inc., PO Box 5100, Carlsbad, CA 92018-5100.
Tel.: (1) 760 431 7695 or (800) 654 5126; Fax: (1) 760 431 6948 or (800) 650 5115.
www.hayhouse.com

Published and distributed in Australia by:
Hay House Australia Ltd, 18/36 Ralph St, Alexandria NSW 2015.
Tel.: (61) 2 9669 4299; Fax: (61) 2 9669 4144.
www.hayhouse.com.au

Published and distributed in the Republic of South Africa by:
Hay House SA (Pty), Ltd, PO Box 990, Witkoppen 2068.
Tel./Fax: (27) 11 467 8904. www.hayhouse.co.za

Published and distributed in India by:
Hay House Publishers India, Muskaan Complex, Plot No.3, B-2,
Vasant Kunj, New Delhi – 110 070. Tel.: (91) 11 4176 1620;
Fax: (91) 11 4176 1630. www.hayhouse.co.in

Distributed in Canada by:
Raincoast, 9050 Shaughnessy St, Vancouver, BC V6P 6E5.
Tel.: (1) 604 323 7100; Fax: (1) 604 323 2600

A catalogue record for this book is available from the British Library.

ISBN: 978-1-84850-824-8

Printed and bound in Great Britain by TJ International Ltd, Padstow, Cornwall

CONTENTS

FOREWORD

There comes a time when any secret will get out into the world. No matter how hard we try to keep it hidden, it will be revealed, made manifest. For centuries, the principles and practices of mindfulness meditation were pretty much hidden away. You had to travel a far distance, perhaps to Asia, to see a teacher who might help you with the inner work of this meditation.

In the 1960s there was some excitement when certain forms of concentration meditation were taught in the West. Western scientists were intrigued: What were the psychological and physiological effects of such practices? The new scientific instruments of the day were used to measure bodily reactions such as heart rate and minor fluctuations in sweating. They showed that these meditations were as effective as deep-relaxation techniques in calming the mind and body, and bringing about states of wellbeing.

But that's as far as it went. Because already-accepted procedures in common use in the West were just as effective, anything 'extra' about the meditation was deemed to be unnecessary. Why recite mantras when identical effects could be found without them? Meditation as a 'technique' for reducing stress was reduced to a minority activity within science, and pursued by a relatively small group of distinguished scientists.

Then something changed. Because we are still living through the effects of this change, we can't be sure exactly what happened, but the dispersion of Tibetan and Vietnamese monks in the second half of the 20th century may lie at its root. The West had been prepared for this, in some ways, from the interest in Zen which had been an important cultural influence in the United States from the 1950s onwards. Also influential were some Westerners who travelled to Asia (especially Thailand and Burma) and brought back a different emphasis – what they called Insight (or Mindfulness) Meditation.

Mindfulness meditation doesn't just emphasize focusing and refocusing attention on a single point, but invites people to combine this training with a receptive, open awareness that might, if cultivated, offer a direct sense of what is arising, moment by moment, in the external and internal world. It also offers a way of responding to these events, and our reactions to them, with open-hearted compassion.

Gradually the message became clearer: we don't need to 'get rid' of our stress, tiredness and sadness, but to see their patterns clearly, and meet them with an open and friendly curiosity. This is different from our habitual reaction, which is to react to something we don't like by either pushing it away or brooding about it. Because we have never been taught any other way to meet our distress, we don't realize how much our habits of avoidance or brooding are making things worse, turning momentary tiredness into exhaustion, momentary fear into chronic worry, and momentary sadness into chronic unhappiness and depression. So it isn't our fault that we end up exhausted, anxious or depressed. We have been given only one tool to deal with things we don't like: get rid of it, work harder, be better, be perfect – and if we fail to make things different, we too easily conclude that we are a failure as a person. This is a recipe for a troubled world. As Jon Kabat-Zinn has said, we need, literally and metaphorically, to come to our senses.

What seems to be changing is that people are grasping this new way of understanding – the way of mindfulness. People are seeing more clearly the origin of much of our suffering, how our own reactions can compound our distress, and the path that can free us. People are returning to some of the original Buddhist texts and, more importantly, the practices that have been passed down over 25 centuries. These, taught in a secular context, have been found in recent scientific studies to liberate people from their stress, anxiety and unhappiness in ways that seem to go beyond the usual results of existing psychological treatments. These studies find that mindfulness not only reduces negative moods and prevents future episodes of clinical depression, but also enhances wellbeing and quality of life, even in the most tragic circumstances, by allowing people to let go of avoidance and brooding, and by cultivating self-compassion.

This is ancient wisdom in the East. But it is a new discovery for the West, and brings with it all the challenges that come when the West 'gets' a 'new thing'. Yet there is something we can say for sure: something that was hidden is now being revealed. We can now grasp it, we can hold it in our hands… and the word for this (from *manus* – hand, and *festus* – grasped) is the familiar word: 'manifesto'.

It is wonderful that Jonty Heaversedge and Ed Halliwell have written this book to give freely of their own experience, and to share the tremendous possibilities that come with training the mind and body to do less and to notice more. Their manifesto, like all manifestos, is both a statement of the potential that lies in all of us and a call to action to realize that potential. In the case of mindfulness, this call to action is to live life, moment by moment, as if it really mattered.

Professor Mark Williams, University of Oxford
Author of *The Mindful Way through Depression*

PREFACE

Meditation is no longer a fringe activity practised by a few new age or spiritual types – it's a widely credited, evidence-based approach to wellbeing. Interest in the subject has grown exponentially – there's been an explosion of academic papers in recent years, feeding increased media coverage and a dramatic rise in the number of clinicians and health centres teaching mindfulness to their patients. Meditation training is also being offered in schools, workplaces and other community settings. More and more people are questioning the cult of speed that dominates our society and are looking for ways to live more contentedly. It seems that mindfulness could offer the ground for fulfilling these aspirations.

Our intention in writing this book is to offer a broad-based introduction to mindfulness, and to make a case for bringing the practice into our lives and our world. We will explore its ancient roots, as well as the increasing scientific basis for its role in optimizing health and wellbeing. We will share stories of people who have benefited from learning to practise meditation, and give guidance on how you can begin to explore the way of mindfulness for yourself. By blending ancient wisdom with modern psychology, immunology and neuroscience, secular with spiritual, empirical with experiential, we've aimed to be as relevant as possible to as many people as possible. We hope you'll find this approach engaging and challenging, and that it will inspire you to explore further.

Mindfulness is a simple, practical and profound way of being that's open to anyone who wishes to engage with it. As such, this isn't a religious book and it's not meant to supplant any faith (or non-faith) tradition that you connect with. We feel, however, that it's important to offer some insight into the origin of these practices in Buddhism, given how far they have emerged from this tradition, even while it's now being presented and validated in a secular, scientific context.

We are only at the beginning of discovering how mindfulness could help us to live happier, more compassionate and more meaningful lives. As well as helping us work with health problems, let go of unskilful behaviours and relate more deeply and compassionately with our jobs, families and friends, we believe it is the basis for knowing and realizing our innate potential as human beings. *The Mindful Manifesto*, then, is not just for people experiencing 'illness'; it is for anyone who wants to be happier and healthier, and to live in a wiser, more peaceful and compassionate world.

Ed Halliwell and Jonty Heaversedge

CHAPTER 1

A CALL TO BEING

Just 'be' for a while – let your attention settle on what's happening in your body, in your mind and the world around you. Be inquisitive about your experience, and slow down enough to notice it.

We live in a restless world. From the moment we open our eyes in the morning, many of us are started on a frantic round of relentless striving that ends only when we crash, exhausted, into bed at night. Whether we're working to earn enough money, build a career, raise kids, help friends or save the planet, it seems we're forever on the go, frenetically trying to propel ourselves to a better future. We're doing, doing, doing – and we get stressed. Around 7 million adults in the UK are so stressed they'd qualify for a diagnosis of anxiety disorder.[1]

There is nothing inherently wrong with doing – after all, it's enabled humanity to achieve some amazing feats. People have created machines that connect us to someone on the other side of the planet. We've made beautiful art, inspiring music, great literature and magnificent architecture. We've accumulated vast storehouses of knowledge that can be used to predict the weather, fly across the sky and carry out heart transplants. In the last 100 years especially, the speed of scientific and technological progress has been astonishing, giving us the capacity to *do* even more, even faster. We can click a mouse, flick a switch or press a button and accomplish tasks that would have taken previous generations many times longer – if they could have managed them at all. Because of all this accomplishment, many of us lead lives that are healthier, safer and more comfortable than our ancestors dared dream of.

But there is a problem. Despite all these amazing advances, are we really content? Isn't the point of all this exertion to make our lives easier, more enjoyable, more fulfilling? Every time someone invents a new app or develops a prescription drug, isn't he or she trying to reduce the amount of hassle or suffering that we have to cope with in our lives? Unfortunately, the evidence speaks for itself: even for those of us who live in the Western world, in countries which boast the highest levels of material comfort, stress is everywhere. Our health services are overwhelmed by patients with chronic illness. We are scared of crime and terrorism. Our relationships break down. Our children don't 'perform' at school. We get into conflict with neighbours. We work too hard, or not enough, or in a job we don't like. While material standards of living have certainly improved over the last century, statistics suggest that we haven't become any happier.[2] Indeed, we seem to be getting more unhappy – the World Health Organization predicts that by the year 2030, depression will have become the planet's biggest health problem.[3]

We are faced with huge global challenges – threats of war, poverty and environmental devastation, for which we have yet to invent a solution. Sometimes our inventions make the suffering even greater. The tremendous technologies of the last century have undoubtedly saved and improved many lives, but they have also been used to kill millions of people, as well as potentially creating a climate catastrophe that threatens our survival as a species.

We want to relieve the stress in our lives and the hardships in our world. We want to be at peace. We want to be more confident, feel safe in our communities, have a good relationship and rewarding career, and we want our children to do well at school. We want to flourish. And so we keep on doing, hoping this will make us feel better. We go to a different doctor, move house, change partners or get a new job – perhaps one that pays more money so we can buy more 'stuff' that might bring us satisfaction. We take pills and potions, bend, stretch, diet and detox. If only we make enough of an effort, surely we can find the solution to our pain? Or maybe we get busy in the other direction, desperately trying to avoid our problems with addictive behaviours like drinking, smoking, overworking, overeating or over-thinking. We drive ourselves to distraction, getting stuck in the mud of our own struggle.

We are not just busy bodies, we are busy minds. When we're not hectically trying to solve our difficulties, we're often consumed with worry or regret. In a recent survey, more than 50 per cent of people said they 'find it difficult to relax or switch off, and can't stop thinking about things I have to do or nagging worries.'[4] When we have an anxious thought, we tend to dwell on it, create a story around it or throw ourselves into a round of punishing criticism: 'I always feel useless compared to Sally, she's so on top of things… mind you, she's boring, she's got no life outside work… oh, great, there I go again, why am I so negative?' Our minds rush hither and thither, brooding about the past and worrying about the future. Even when we say we're 'doing nothing', we're often trying to drown out our thoughts in the chatter of the TV.

Some of us decide we want to do something to relieve not just our own suffering, but that of the world. We want to cure cancer, so we become a doctor. We want to beat crime, so we join the police. We want to stop global warming, famine and war, so we recycle our plastic bags, give money to charity or go on marches. As the saying goes: 'Don't just sit there, do something.' A few people want to do something so much that they go into politics. They devise and carry out programmes designed to solve our problems – improving the lot of communities, countries or even the planet through determined programmes of reform.

But what if all this striving to make things better is actually part of the problem? What if our compulsive habit of *doing* is actually part of the reason we're so miserable? What if, rather than needing to take *more* action, we need to take *less*? What if we don't need technology to speed up, but ourselves to slow down?

One of the frequently heard cries from 21st-century citizens is for some 'headspace'. No wonder – there's precious little space in our minds, and precious little space in our lives. The faster we go, the less room we have for reflection and the more we tend to act impulsively, following unconscious habitual patterns that aren't good for us.

In our multitasking age, we cram so much into our lives that not much gets our undivided attention. We get so obsessed with trying to achieve ten things at once that we're rarely fully present for any one of them. In our struggle to get ahead and reach our goals, we fail to inhabit the moment, here and now.

Even the devices designed to help us get things done faster (and therefore give us more time) actually end up making us feel more anxious.[5] Information bombards us from every direction – we walk around with our headphones in, send text messages to one friend while chatting to another, answer the phone when we're eating a meal, and reply to office e-mails from the beach.

The increasing amount of time we spend online may be changing the neural pathways in our brains, making us less able to pay attention to or absorb anything in depth.[6] We are more likely to skim the surface of experience – flitting helplessly from one stimulus to the next. Ironically, in an era of 'connectivity', being in constant contact can disconnect us from the people around us if we relate with them only at surface level.

Relentless speed and distraction lead us into a kind of semi-existence: we get stuck in a conceptual world of thinking about what we want to achieve, and what we want to avoid, rather than experiencing where we actually are. It looks like we're here, but we're not really showing up for our lives. By shutting ourselves off from the full range of our experience – internal and external – we miss important feedback from our bodies and our environment. Swept away by our thoughts and feelings, we end up perpetuating our stress, pulled unawares into repeating cycles of behaviour that keep us unhappy.

Stress itself can make us ill. Problems like depression and anxiety feature in around 30 per cent of the average family doctor's caseload,[7] and at least another third relate to stress-related 'medically unexplained' symptoms that are difficult to diagnose or treat effectively.[8] We don't like feeling powerless, and so we often react to these problems with further struggle – desperately searching for a new drug or treatment, a new specialist or diagnosis. Unfortunately, because striving is frequently a cause of the illness, this can actually make things worse.

Most of us know that the way we react to difficulty isn't always helpful. When someone actually stops and asks what makes us feel better, we are prompted to reflect and respond wisely. Eighty-one per cent of us agree that 'the fast pace of life and the number of things we have to do and worry about these days is a major cause of stress, unhappiness and illness in our society', while 86 per cent agree that 'people would be much happier and healthier if they knew how to slow down and live in the moment'.[9]

But the cult of achievement is all around us, making its lure difficult to resist. From the day we were born, we hear that taking our foot off the gas is lazy. We may have learned this from our parents, who were probably busy trying to succeed while we were growing up, and from our schools, which often teach that the way to survive in a busy world is to get busy ourselves. And we learn it from the media, which provides a constant stream of news, entertainment and drama, reminding us how other people are getting things done – especially influential ones like politicians, sportspeople and celebrities. If we're busy, the message goes, we can become rich, and if we're rich we can afford things that will make us happy. We see those around us in the hunt for possessions and status, and feel impelled to try and match them. These messages imprint themselves on our thoughts and behaviour, even when they make us miserable. So we just keep on going, keep on doing, even though we know, deep down, there's something wrong.

Even if we were to try and change these patterns, how would we manage it? Gripped by the desire for instant gratification, we tend to want answers in quick-fix form – a magic pill to remove our misery, a miracle diet to sort our weight problem, a fast-acting therapy to free us from past conditioning. But quick-fix solutions don't usually work, because we're attempting to solve our problems using the same mind-set that created them. Accelerating is not the solution when we're already going too fast – it's like putting your foot on the gas instead of applying the brakes.

So, maybe we need to let go of solutions for a while, and look instead at how we're trying to reach them. If simply striving for a happier life were the answer, wouldn't it have worked by now? Perhaps it's time to take a different approach, one that invites us to slow down and pay more attention to how we experience our lives, and what drives us, before we start trying to make changes. Maybe we first need to learn how to be, just where we are, rather than always trying to get somewhere else. If we could give ourselves permission to be, perhaps we might discover what, if anything, we need to do.

LEARNING TO *BE*

Giving yourself permission to *be* – doing less and noticing more – is what the Mindful Manifesto is really about. It isn't the usual kind of manifesto – there's no great plan to solve all our problems instantly. Instead, it's an invitation to let go of doing, at least for a time, and learn how to *be*, right now, in the present moment.

The word 'manifesto' derives from the Latin verb *manifestare*, which means 'to show plainly'. In English, to manifest means 'to become apparent'. Our suggestion is that by learning how to *be*, we might start to release a deep wisdom that can show us plainly how things really are, and that this might naturally create the ground for knowing what to do. Things can become apparent, our deepest values can become clear, and we can begin to act with greater wisdom.

By using the word 'manifesto' in this way, we are reclaiming its true meaning – not a plan of action, but a call to being. By learning how to be, we take our foot off the accelerator, come out of overdrive and restore some balance to our lives. Rather than desperately searching for a cure to our problems, we begin to let a natural wakefulness emerge. We stop seeking answers, and let them come to us. We give up the fight – *and* the stress that comes with it.

Learning how to *be* could make a real difference to our happiness, not just as individuals, but as couples, families, communities, nations – and as a planet. Whether it's relationship issues, an unhealthy addiction or the threat of war, we create space for choices to emerge. As the dust created by our stress begins to settle, we might open up and relax into our situation. A new kind of wisdom may start to dawn, and we can begin to manifest more creatively, decisively and appropriately.

It sounds simple, doesn't it? And in a sense, it is – if we can really be present to the here and now, we might start to relate with our lives in a more harmonious way. Unfortunately, although it is simple, manifesting like this isn't easy. Try it for yourself and perhaps you'll see what we mean. For the next two minutes, put this book down and rest your mind and body in the present moment. Don't try to *do* anything – just allow yourself to *be*.

THE HABIT OF BUSYNESS

So, how was it? Maybe you were confused ('I'm not sure what I'm supposed to be doing – should something be happening here?'), irritated ('What a pointless exercise! Of course I know how to be – I'm being all the time, aren't I?'), or excited ('Ah great, we're getting to the part where they tell me how to sort out all my issues!')? Perhaps you got interrupted by someone who thought you were acting strangely, or who desperately wanted you to talk to them. Maybe you got irritated by the noise of a car and started thinking about how you wished it was quieter. Perhaps you got caught up worrying that you'd left the gas on. Or maybe you got fidgety and felt compelled to go and make a cup of coffee. Or you didn't do the exercise at all – you couldn't wait to get onto the next paragraph, or just couldn't be bothered. Whatever happened, you probably didn't instantly find yourself feeling naturally wise, open and relaxed, spontaneously in tune with your world (if you did, then congratulations, you probably don't need this book!).

Why *is* 'being' so difficult for most of us? Surely it shouldn't be so hard simply to dwell in the here and now, if only for two minutes? It's difficult because we aren't used to it. We've practised doing and distraction for much of our lives, and the constant pressures from around us keep the habit in place. It's even part of our biology – these patterns of behaviour are hardwired into us through millions of years of evolution. In order to release ourselves, we need help. We need an antidote. We need a method.

THE METHOD OF MINDFULNESS

That method is mindfulness. With mindfulness, we train in paying attention, noticing what's happening in our body, our thoughts and emotions, as well as the world around us. By working with simple meditation practices, we deliberately and gently bring more awareness – more 'being' – into our experience. Gradually, as we pay attention, we begin to notice how we get caught up on automatic pilot, unconsciously playing out patterns that create stress and suffering in our lives. As we practise this new way of relating, we can gradually start to free ourselves from these outmoded habits.

To practise mindfulness, we let go of action for a while and just watch what happens, with curiosity and friendliness. We see how everything arises and passes away, and how we don't have to get so caught up in everything – we can observe it all in a friendly, compassionate and interested way. We begin to see that we aren't our thoughts and feelings, and that they don't have to dominate us – we learn that we can stop taking things so personally. We start to see the possibility of living more lightly, and the weight on our shoulders can begin to lift. We discover the foundation for a kinder and more confident relationship with ourselves, with others and with life.

In mindfulness, we learn to tolerate our impulse to follow patterns that don't serve us. We cultivate a gap between thought and action, and gradually, as we become more skilled in our practice, the ability to dwell in this gap grows and we are impelled less and less into knee-jerk reactions. We can stay with our experience long enough to consider our options. We can step out of automatic pilot.

Practising mindfulness means giving up the search for instant answers that come from outside of us. It means taking a profound, radical step, starting to work with suffering in the heart of our own experience. This is supremely empowering – for, while we may not appear to have full control over external events, we can always work with our mind, gently, firmly and repeatedly training ourselves to thrive in the midst of life's challenges. In undertaking this inner work, we aren't just tinkering with what job we do, where we live, how much money we make or whom we decide to be friends with – we are changing how we relate with our consciousness, the faculty that actually experiences what we do. This means that whatever happens to us, we have the tools for wellbeing more squarely in our own hands.

It's a bit like having a TV with a fuzzy picture – it blurs, cuts out and there's snow on the screen. You try changing channels, fiddling with the remote, switching it on and off again or kicking it. Finally you call the technician, who goes up on the roof and shifts the aerial – it had been forced out of place by the wind. Your reception becomes clear.

Many of us deal with our problems in the same way: we try to change channels, hit the remote or kick the TV – struggling to alter the contents of our lives. When we practise mindfulness, we're learning how to change the position of our aerial, to see things from a different perspective. We're training ourselves to receive experience more accurately and fully.

This way of being – the way of mindfulness – is nothing new. It has been advocated and practised by wise men and women for thousands of years. Many millions of people have tried it and found that it helps them – they report that they start to become gentler, more centred, more connected, more alive. From a ground of greater being, they report a beneficial shift in the way they relate to their lives.

Unfortunately, although this wisdom has been around for millennia, it has not been widely known or practised in our culture. Meditation has often been dismissed as something to do with exotic Eastern religions or crackpot new-age spirituality. All that's fine for alternative types, people sometimes say, but a waste of time for us regular folk. The possibility that mindfulness could help us cope with the demands of the modern world has been sadly ignored.

MINDFULNESS IN THE MAINSTREAM

That is, until now. In recent years, powerful people have started to sit up and take notice. They are starting to see that it might be a way to work with some of the enormous problems we face as a world. The subject is no longer discussed only on the spiritual fringes, in self-help sections of bookshops and alternative health centres – it's being advocated by doctors, health policy-makers and politicians. Almost one in ten of us already practise meditation,[10] and many more are expressing an interest. At last, mindfulness is being taken seriously. It is going mainstream.

So why is this happening now? After all, practitioners have been saying for thousands of years that meditation leads to greater wellbeing, and yet nobody has much listened. Are we finally recognizing the impact of our lifestyles, noticing how out of balance we've become? In a world dominated by speed, aggression and absent-mindedness, are we intuitively sensing that we need more stillness and presence in our lives?

Perhaps so. But there's another driver for the attention being given to mindfulness these days – and that is *science*. In recent years, a large and ever-growing volume of research on the subject has accumulated, testing some of the claims that are made for its effectiveness. Pioneering practitioners and researchers have developed new programmes based on meditation and carefully examined them to see if they work. It started with a trickle of studies in the 1980s and 1990s, but since the turn of the millennium this trickle has swelled into a tide. Around 300 to 400 scientific papers on mindfulness are now being published each year, and the evidence is showing it can help with a very wide range of issues.[11]

What does the data tell us? First, it indicates that mindfulness can help us cope with stress, anxiety and depression, influencing our psychological health in a host of positive ways. It can help us let go of negative thought patterns, improve our quality of life and nurture self-esteem and emotional balance. The research also shows that practising mindfulness can help us sharpen our attention, concentration and memory.

Second, the research suggests that mindfulness can play an important role in helping us look after our physical health – strengthening the immune system, speeding up healing and helping people cope with a wide range of common and debilitating illnesses, including chronic pain, cancer and diabetes.

Third, studies show that mindfulness can help us let go of unskilful patterns of behaviour – it can be used in the management of eating disorders and substance abuse, to improve sleep and to offer balance when we get carried away by anger and other powerful emotions.

Fourth, the science suggests that mindfulness can help us relate with others more effectively. Studies have shown, for example, that it can help us enjoy more satisfying and empathic relationships, fostering creativity and compassion in our dealings with people at home, at school, at work or in our other communities.

Researchers have also found that practising mindfulness can lead to changes in the brain and body that seem to reflect these reports of greater wellbeing. Meditation seems to increase activity and even promote growth in neural networks associated with positive attitudes, and to reduce activity in areas of the brain associated with distress. It appears to help us regulate our nervous system and reduce stress hormone levels. Whereas the distractions of our 21st-century technology may be altering our brains and bodies in harmful ways, the ancient inner technology of meditation seems to foster helpful biological shifts.

Studies have also found that people who are more naturally mindful are less neurotic, less defensive and more extroverted than less mindful people, as well as having more energy and awareness and being generally happier with their lives. When they do experience sad moods, they recover from them more quickly. Mindful people care about others – they feel closer to and more connected with them – as well as being kinder to the planet, acting in more environmentally friendly ways.

We live in a scientific age, and when this kind of research demonstrates that something is beneficial, people take it seriously. That's understandable – the scientific method has led to many of the great achievements of the 'doing' world over the past few centuries, especially in areas such as medicine and health. When a few spiritual devotees or new-age dropouts said that meditation was helpful, they were never going to convince the mainstream. But when reputable academics from universities like Harvard and Oxford start saying the same thing, and providing the numbers to prove it, that's something very different.

WHAT IS MINDFULNESS?

Trying to define mindfulness is tricky. Definitions can be helpful, but they can also be somewhat misleading. Take the ideas of mindfulness that have long been used in the English language: we talk about being mindful of someone else's feelings, of pedestrians crossing a busy road, or the step as we get off the train. While mindfulness in this sense has something to do with paying attention, and taking care, it isn't the whole of what we mean here.

The definition often used in courses which teach mindfulness is 'paying attention in a particular way: on purpose, in the present moment, and non-judgementally'. In this case, mindfulness seems to refer not just generally to being careful, but to a deliberate, unbiased quality of awareness that connects us to the here and now. But this still doesn't really show us how to foster this kind of attention, or what it might be like to experience it.

At other times, we might hear mindfulness talked about in terms of meditation practice – in this instance it seems to involve sitting or lying down and resting our attention on our breathing, a particular phrase or our thoughts. So is that what mindfulness is?

The problem with approaching mindfulness as a concept to be defined is that we inevitably end up thinking about it and, while we're doing that, it remains just an idea rather than an experience. As one traditional image has it, words are like 'fingers pointing at the moon' – guiding us where to look, but not something we should mistake for the moon itself.

Visualize a 'banana' – would the description 'yellow, mushy fruit' give you much of a sense of 'banana' if you had never come across one before? A little, perhaps, but certainly not as much as seeing and tasting a banana for yourself – you might assume it was similar to another fruit that fits that description and which you *have* come across – a mango, perhaps. Your idea of 'banana' would be inaccurate, based on your preconceptions, until you came into direct contact with one. Even then, it would only be that banana, in that moment. Our idea of 'banana' is based on all our previous experiences of bananas – it can never fully describe the experience of sensing each unique fruit when we encounter it. The words and concepts are a poor substitute for the experience.

It's the same with mindfulness – our ideas are bound to be inaccurate unless we experience it for ourselves. This is perhaps especially pertinent with mindfulness because the word actually refers to the direct experience of things, free from our preconceived ideas about them. The word mindfulness is a concept about transcending our tendency to conceptualize – no wonder trying to describe it is confusing! If we really want to understand mindfulness, we have to try it out, to engage in it, to practise it. Words can't do it justice.

Perhaps another useful analogy would be learning to play the piano – we can read as many books about piano-playing as we like, but until we actually sit down in front of a keyboard and start playing, preferably under the guidance of a good teacher, we won't know what sounds we can produce. Similarly with mindfulness: we can read about 'being' all we like, but until we actually practise it, our realization of how it can help us is likely to be limited.

As we have already found, attempting to 'be' isn't easy. Like sitting down in front of a piano without having had any lessons, the result might not be all that harmonious. Fortunately, over thousands of years simple means have been developed to help us connect with being, and to train our awareness. This is meditation practice, and it works on mindfulness just like taking lessons in a musical instrument helps us to play.

We'll be offering guidance on how to practise meditation in the chapters that follow, as well as pointers to other ways you can seek out mindfulness instruction. In the meantime, here are some words that might begin to offer you a flavour of mindfulness. Don't analyse them too much, or worry if they don't seem to make sense right now – remember, these descriptions are just like fingers pointing at the moon: they may help you recognize mindfulness when you experience it, but they can never replace the experience itself.

- Mindfulness means observing things just as they are – our thoughts, emotions, body sensations and what's happening in the world around us. It shows us the world just as a mirror reflects images: clearly, openly and without bias. It's what happens when the mind watches and engages consciously with life, rather than being blindly caught up in what's going on.

- Mindfulness is a way of experiencing the world through our senses, intuitively rather than through the filter of thought. It connects us to experiential understanding, penetrating into the heart of things, beyond the stories we spin about our lives.

- Mindfulness is intentional, energetic, careful and precise. It is also accepting, gentle, spacious and kind.

- Mindfulness is an ABC skill: it helps us train in becoming more aware (A) and in 'being with' our experience (B) rather than reacting to it impulsively. This gives us more choice (C) about how we relate with situations in our lives.

- Mindfulness brings the mind and body together, in balance and flow. In some Eastern philosophies the mind is said to be located not in the head but in the heart – mindfulness can thus be thought of as 'heartfulness'. It is an attitude of warmth, friendliness and compassion, to oneself and to others.

- Mindfulness means leaning into life (even when it's painful), approaching experiences with interest, curiosity and courage. It also means relating to experience with equanimity, as it's from this ground of acceptance that we can act consciously and decisively, unfettered by our habitual patterns of judging, labelling and reacting.

- Mindfulness is coming to know yourself, inside out, outside in. It is knowing what you are doing, when you're doing it. Mindfulness is being awake to life, rather than sleepwalking through it.

- Mindfulness is the act of remembering to pay attention – it's the opposite of automatic pilot, the mode in which we just blindly follow our habits, not fully present to what's going on. When we're on automatic pilot, we might drive down the motorway and miss our turn because we're caught up thinking about something else. When we are driving mindfully, we're fully present to the experience of driving – aware of the road, the car, our thoughts and feelings about the journey, other drivers and so on.

- Mindfulness means relating to our thoughts as just thoughts, our feelings as just feelings, our actions as just actions – they are not the whole of who we are. Mindfulness comes from a deeper awareness that is not caught up in our thoughts and feelings, although it can see them and work with them effectively. Mindfulness means relating *to* our experience rather than just *from* our experience.

Mindfulness is simple to learn, and yet it can help with so many different problems. It can be used on the bus, in the supermarket, at your desk or in bed. You don't need any special equipment – just your mind and body. And while proficiency takes practice, you don't need to spend years meditating in an ashram or monastery to make a difference – less than a week's practice of 20 minutes a day can be enough to start producing measurable shifts.[12] And from the smallest daily quibbles to the largest global problems, there probably isn't any circumstance where more mindfulness wouldn't be beneficial.

Because of all the scientific research, this news is starting to reach some of the people who need it most. In the United States, mindfulness is already being taught in many hospitals, to people with conditions ranging from anxiety, fatigue and back pain to heart disease, HIV and cancer. In the UK, mindfulness is recommended in the National Health Service as a treatment for people who have experienced repeated episodes of depression. GPs are becoming much more convinced of its value for their patients,[13] and programmes have been set up to teach mindfulness to people with addictions, to pregnant women and their partners, to schoolchildren and to couples who want to enjoy better relationships.

Encouraged by the results so far, more scientists are entering the field, and more funding bodies are willing to back studies in what is starting to be considered a respectable area of study. Between 2008 and 2010, the US National Institutes of Health alone granted 102 awards ranging up to $1.2 million in size for mindfulness research.[14]

Because mindfulness seems to be such a helpful way of working with stress, it can be applied in a whole range of contexts – stress, after all, is everywhere. From day-to-day home and work demands to debilitating diseases and depression, from our personal problems and conflicts to international issues like war or climate change, stress makes everything worse. If mindfulness can help us manage our stress better, it can help us manage everything better.

The mindful approach is now quite well known and respected among health professionals, but when we consider the number of people suffering from anxiety, depression and chronic physical ill-health, the services available are little more than a drop in the ocean. The same is true in schools, workplaces and prisons – there are exciting pilot schemes, but many people still probably aren't aware of how mindfulness could help.

That's why we have decided to write this book. In *The Mindful Manifesto*, we'd like to invite you to learn more about mindfulness through an exploration of its history, philosophy, science and practice. We'd like to invite you to see how it could make a difference – in your own life, and to our stressed-out world. And we'd like to invite you to begin practising mindfulness with us – to step off the treadmill of doing and distraction and to investigate this way of being. We don't promise instant results – indeed, if the practice is to work, we'll have to let go of goal-oriented craving and the need for quick solutions. But if we can do that, we might be able to relax and enjoy the journey.

We'll start by exploring where mindfulness has come from – its roots in spiritual practices dating back thousands of years, and its role as a lynchpin of ancient Buddhist teachings on how to relieve suffering. Then, in the following chapter we'll describe how this practice came to the West in the late 20th century and was adapted to help patients suffering from chronic illness. We'll examine how mindfulness affects the body, and how practising it can reduce our stress levels and help us cope with physical health problems.

Then we'll tell the story of how psychologists working in mental health discovered mindfulness in the mid-1990s, and how their 'new' treatment has had remarkable success in helping people to cope with depression. We'll also look at how the ancient teachings on mindfulness connect with modern neuroscientific research that suggests meditation can alter the way our brain works, and even its physical structure.

Next, we'll show how mindfulness can be used to help treat addictions, and how anyone can develop a greater ability to let go of destructive behaviours. And we'll suggest how mindfulness can help us to be more effective and happy in other aspects of our lives, such as at work and in relationships. And finally we'll look at the big picture – how mindfulness can facilitate a saner approach to social problems and help us meet the myriad challenges of our age.

All the way through we'll be sharing our own experiences, as well as the stories of people whose lives have been touched and helped by mindfulness. We'll also offer tips and suggestions on how you can begin to develop your own meditation practice – giving you a taste of the experience and pointing you to ways of investigating further.

Practising mindfulness isn't always a comfortable experience. We rely on routine and find comfort in habitual patterns of behaviour that we've rehearsed for most of our lives. They won't disappear overnight. Meditation practice requires patience, discipline and energy, as well as gentleness and compassion. Sometimes it may seem frustrating, boring or confusing – and sometimes it may seem like nothing much is happening at all. We may still get caught up in our hopes, our fears and our speed, and we may still be impelled towards old habits. It can be painful to see and experience these habits so clearly, to face our difficulties squarely rather than trying to ignore or escape from them.

But if we are motivated, a fresh perspective can begin to develop. By practising regularly, and without striving for results, our minds and bodies can start to loosen up and our habits can weaken their grip on us. We can start to be present more often – to become more confident, open and relaxed. We can start to be, as well as to do.

Before we go any further, we thought it might be helpful to share how we became confident about the power of mindfulness. First, there is our professional experience. As a GP and a mindfulness teacher, we both see people suffering from illnesses that are either caused or made worse by stress. We have become conscious of how the pressures of our world are at the root of so much of the pain and suffering we witness. We have studied the scientific research, and we've also seen people who are enormously helped by learning how to practise meditation – their anxiety levels falling, their conditions becoming more manageable and their ability to thrive increasing, despite often very serious health problems.

Above all, we have benefited from mindfulness ourselves. We both experience the pressure to do, achieve and consume that is endemic in our society, and we're vulnerable to that pressure, and the stress it creates. We both find that mindfulness is a powerful antidote – not a miracle cure, but a way of working with experience that's both simple and effective. Below is a short summary of how each of us came to this conclusion, and how it continues to work in and on our lives.

Jonty's Experience

I first came across mindfulness and meditation about nine years ago. I had just turned 30 and there was a lot to celebrate. I was progressing well in a fulfilling career as a GP, I had good friends and no particular financial concerns. I should have felt a sense of achievement, but instead, in my mind I felt stuck. I was unhappy and didn't know why.

I didn't feel like I was depressed and I knew I didn't need medication, but I also realized that I needed help to untangle the knot my mind was in. I started seeing a psychotherapist who was very helpful but, as therapy came to an end, I felt I wanted to find some ongoing way of working with my mind. So I began to investigate meditation.

Like most people, when I first heard about meditation I made a whole range of assumptions – and my friends all joked about the idea of me sitting cross-legged and eating lentils (neither of which is necessary to practise being mindful!). For me the biggest resistance I had was to its origins in Buddhism. I had no real understanding of Buddhist philosophy, but I was worried about getting involved in anything 'religious'. As a GP I try to take a scientific approach to life and, while I respect people from all faiths and traditions, I wanted something that I could question and that could offer me some *evidence* of its benefits – both personally and professionally.

I was lucky enough to find the Shambhala Meditation Centre in London. As well as Buddhist programmes, it also offered a more secular approach to meditation, and the teachers there were completely open to my process of exploration. While psychotherapy was the first step in changing my relationship with myself, meditation has offered me a very practical technique for continued observation and reflection in my life. I would still not say that I am 'a Buddhist', but the knowledge and wisdom I have encountered throughout this process have provided a structure that has not only helped me calm my mind, but also to understand more about its nature… something that offers me great reassurance as I continue to notice more and more of my neurotic tendencies!

I haven't become a new person. I am, however, more able to notice how I think and what I do, and the impact this has on me and the people around me. The biggest difference is that I do this with more compassion and humour, and less judgement and self-criticism than I used to. I am able to be inquisitive about my life without feeling driven to try and solve every problem I encounter, and without feeding the constant cycle of self-improvement I so easily get trapped in.

Initially I found meditation uncomfortable, both mentally and physically. Just sitting still, noticing and letting go was so different from my usual energetic, solution-focused approach to life. I found the practice frustrating (and still do a lot of the time). However, as time passed I began to notice differences in the way I handled situations at work, in my confidence with relationships and, most wonderfully of all, in my ability to connect with my patients. I was able to be more attentive and available to them in consultations as I became less distracted by all the other thoughts jockeying for my attention. As I started to meditate regularly I found myself more able to be present in every situation that I encountered, both in and out of work.

This is not always an easy experience – mindfulness allows us to start seeing things as they are rather than as we would like them to be. But it also enables us to bring our intelligence and our heart to bear in whatever situation comes our way. This offers me the opportunity to remove my metaphorical blinkers, and to be more creative, equitable and compassionate in my responses, rather than simply reacting with my usual habitual defensiveness to new challenges.

I have seen how helpful these practices have been in my life – in my ability to take care of myself, my patients, my family and my friends. It has given me the courage to say yes to things I would previously have been too frightened to agree to (whether it's involved appearing on TV in front of millions of people or even writing a book), and to say no to things I would usually feel too insecure to refuse.

. . . .

Ed's Experience

Learning how to practise meditation was the turning point that led me to recovery from a period of chronic depression and anxiety that lasted nearly three years. After working speedily and mindlessly in a media career that brought plenty of material benefits, I'd suddenly collapsed under the weight of stress. Signed off work, I was miserable and frightened. I thought the way to deal with my problems was to *do* something. And at that point I was so anxious that I was willing to try anything.

Within a few months, I had enough psychology and self-help books to start a small library. I was seeing a therapist, taking antidepressants, attending support groups and seminars, and having all sorts of alternative treatments. I tried changing friends, changing jobs, changing where I lived – but none of it seemed to make much difference. In fact, it just made me feel more powerless. By seeking answers with the desperate distraction that had led to my crisis, I was perpetuating the same old patterns – if only I could just keep trying harder, I thought, I would be able to shake myself into a happier future.

In among all my books were some about meditation. People suggested it might be helpful for me, so I went to a local centre that offered instruction. Initially, I approached the practice in the same way as all my other 'fixes' – throwing myself at it in the hope that I had finally found the answer. But there's something very clever about meditation – it's impossible to follow the instructions properly and chase after results at the same time. Soon, it dawned on me – it was not so much *what* I was doing that was the problem, as *how* my mind worked – it was going way too hard, way too fast. In meditation, I saw my habitual patterns of speed and distraction for the first time. I let go – at least a little bit. After a few months of meditating every day, my depression and anxiety began to lift.

I'm still prone to overdoing it, and to getting depressed, so I've continued to practise – habitual patterns can be persistent. But gradually, the bouts of mental ill-health that used to be so regular and debilitating have begun to diminish, both in frequency and duration.

. . . .

CHAPTER 2

MINDFULNESS OF BREATHING

Take some time every day to be mindful of your breath – touch in with the remarkable experience of being alive.

Are you aware of your breathing? We mean, are you *really* aware of the *experience* of breathing, right now, in your body? Not the thought, 'Yes, of course I'm breathing,' but the actual sensation of breath circulating through your body in this very moment? Are you aware of the air brushing lightly against the inside of your nostrils as you breathe in? Do you notice the rising of your chest as your lungs fill with air? Can you feel the expansion of your abdomen as the breath flows down into your belly? How about the beating of your heart – are you able to sense it pumping oxygenated blood through your body? Now, are you aware of your breath as you exhale, the contraction of the belly and the dropping down of your chest, the cool breeze under your nose or on your lips as the air mixes once more with the space around you?

See if you can pay attention to your breathing like this for a few moments. Really connect with your breath, not as an intellectual idea, but through feeling it, touching into it. Be curious about your experience. Whereabouts do you feel these sensations? What are their qualities? There's no need to analyse – just noticing is fine. Whenever you find that your attention has wandered away from the breath – you suddenly find yourself caught up in thinking, perhaps about what you had for breakfast this morning, the ache in your stomach, or what a weird exercise this is – just notice that your mind has wandered and gently bring it back, so that your attention is resting on your breath once more. This is the practice of mindful breathing.

Isn't the breath amazing? All day and night, our body keeps on breathing, whether we are conscious of it or not. Even when we fall asleep, we're drawing in air, filling our lungs, feeding our organs – our breathing keeps us alive. We don't need to do anything; we can just allow it to happen. Our bodies breathe for us. It's wonderful.

How often do you pay attention to your breathing in this way? And how often, on the other hand, do you just take it for granted, assuming that your body will keep you alive simply because that's what it's been doing all your life?

Breathing is the most basic activity we engage in as living creatures. When we stop doing it for more than a few minutes, we die. And yet most of us rarely check in with this vital process – we rarely notice how it feels, on the most fundamental bodily level, to be alive.

If we hardly ever notice the texture, the quality, the feel of our breathing – a process that's happening in us all the time – then what else are we missing? What other experiences routinely pass us by, perhaps because we are busy thinking about the past or the future, or trying to get somewhere other than where we actually are? How much of our lives do we spend on automatic pilot?

We might discover a lot more about ourselves and the world around us if we were able to pay more attention to each moment, in the same way that we just paid attention to our breathing. There's ordinary magic around us: in the majesty of a tree, for example, perhaps one that has stood for hundreds of years, and whose living parts – leaves, branches and trunk – are all as miraculous and mysterious as our own bodies. Wonder is found across the natural world: in the insects and rodents that crawl or scurry about beneath us, and in the stars and sun, those giant formations which nevertheless form only a tiny speck of this universe that we really know so little about.

Perhaps we could pay more attention to our own achievements, too – sensing the ingredients in a delicious meal, savouring the exquisite taste as we roll the food around with our tongue? Perhaps we could look up at the buildings in our street, and see how, brick upon brick, they've been carefully constructed, and how they shelter us from the elements? Perhaps we could even pay attention to the cursor on a computer screen, noticing how it darts about when we shift an electronic mouse from side to side. How many of us fully understand how and why this remarkable piece of technology works, or how it came to be invented?

AN ANCIENT PRACTICE

Becoming more aware in this way – with mindfulness – has been recommended throughout history as a means to unlocking a fresher, deeper perspective, turning us towards a saner way of life. Socrates warned us to 'beware the barrenness of a busy life', declaring that 'wisdom begins in wonder' and even that 'the unexamined life is not worth living'. 'Search your heart and see,' urged the Chinese sage Lao Tzu, 'the way to do is to be.'

Franz Kafka also understood that joy can come to us if we simply rest in our experience. 'You do not need to leave your room,' he suggested. 'Remain sitting at your table and listen. Do not even listen, simply wait. The world will freely offer itself to you to be unmasked, it has no choice – it will roll in ecstasy at your feet.' The potential value of this exercise was noted by the French mathematician Pascal – he suggested that 'most of the problems of the world would be solved if people could learn to sit quietly in a room'.[1]

Fortunately, there are meditation practices which can help us open up to this wider perspective, offering a way of training in being still and paying attention. Human beings have been meditating as far back as records go – there are descriptions of yogic techniques in Hindu texts that were written around 2000–3000 BC. And they were probably practising well before that – it's been suggested that early men and women may have found themselves in a state of meditation when they gazed in wonder at the flickering flames of a fire.

Meditation has appeared in cultures across the world, and in every age. Often it has taken the form of spiritual practice, such as in Christianity, Judaism, Islam or shamanic rituals, a way of connecting with a deeper experience of reality. But even if you aren't religious, you've probably experienced moments in your life when you've felt really present to yourself, to other people or to the environment – in the arms of a lover, perhaps, or standing by the sea. In these moments we feel connected, in touch with our body, mind and world. The psychologist Abraham Maslow called them 'peak experiences', and while they can happen naturally, they may start to occur more often when people practise meditation (although, as we will discover, they can't be sought after).

The root of the word 'meditation' is the Indo-European *med*, which means 'to measure'. By noticing something in a meditative way, we are both taking its measure and doing so in a measured way. We are watching something non-judgementally, with awareness and equanimity, aspiring to see it as it really is rather than buying into the projections our minds habitually add to the experience.

A MANIFOLD PRACTICE

The word 'meditation' can refer to a wide range of practices. Some involve repetition or contemplation of a word or phrase, some make use of visualization, while others are based more on physical movement, such as in martial arts or yoga. The Latin word *meditatio* originally meant any kind of exercise, physical or mental. While not all meditation practices are mindfulness meditations, most of them involve paying attention to an object of some kind, and as such are likely to foster mindfulness.

The mindfulness practices we are exploring in this book – including the mindfulness of breathing exercise at the start of this chapter – are often associated with an Indian prince called Siddhartha Gautama, who lived 2,500 years ago. Although born into great privilege, and despite his father showering him with luxury, Siddhartha eventually realized that the riches of the world couldn't save him, or anyone else, from the inevitable pains of human life – from the suffering associated with growing old, sickness and death, and with other kinds of loss and change. Realizing that there must be another way, he decided to leave the material comforts of his royal palace and seek liberation from the discontent that accompanies so much of our existence.

The story goes that, after studying with a number of teachers, and a further period of training in isolation, Siddhartha declared that he had found a way out of anguish. For the next 45 years, he taught his methods to those who also sought release from their suffering. Siddhartha became known as the Buddha, which means the Awakened One, and he spent the rest of his life showing others how to access this same sense of freedom and peace.

With its institutional forms, spiritual leaders and scriptures, Buddhism is often considered to be one of the world's great religions. But if he were alive today, the Buddha might well be considered a psychologist rather than a religious leader, and his instructions would probably be considered a form of psychotherapy. While there are elements of Buddhism that may seem religious, its essential teachings are focused on handling life in the here and now – a process of investigation leading to insight about how things are, rather than a system of beliefs about what may be. It's a pragmatic approach to life that asks 'What is the nature of things?' and 'How can we live our lives well?'

The Buddha discouraged his students from metaphysical speculation about the hereafter. He also advised them not to trust what he said on faith alone, or on the basis of religious authority or scripture. The only true test of his teaching, he said, was whether it resonated with their own experience. When they put it into practice, was it helpful for them?

THE FOUR NOBLE TRUTHS

At the core of these teachings are a series of observations called The Four Noble Truths. These four truths give a concise diagnosis of the trials of human life, and a prescription for how they can fruitfully be worked with.

The first truth seems obvious – that as human beings we experience suffering. We are born, we get ill, we die and, in between, we undergo all kinds of physical and mental pain. Our bodies go wrong, wear out and eventually fall apart, and our minds are often in turmoil – we get angry, upset, frightened and depressed. No matter how rich we are, how well-toned our bodies or how mentally balanced, we still experience a basic level of stress, disappointment and dissatisfaction that seems to come with the territory of being human.

The Buddha's second noble truth is that there is a root cause for this suffering. We're troubled not so much because we experience the inconveniences of life, but because we constantly want *not* to experience them – we crave, cling to and chase after pleasure and we try to resist and escape discomfort. We don't want to face ageing, sickness and death, even though these and life's other unpalatable difficulties are part and parcel of being human. We try to hold on to pleasurable experiences, and avoid, blank out or distract ourselves from painful ones. We cling to the way we *wish* things were, and resist how they *actually* are.

In one memorable analogy, the Buddha said that our experience of suffering was a bit like being struck by two arrows. When we're hit with the first arrow, rather than thinking that this is unpleasant enough, we then shoot ourselves with another one. The first arrow is the unavoidable pain of life, and the second is all the mental and emotional anguish we heap on top of it.

So it isn't pain itself that causes our suffering, so much as our attempts to avoid difficult experiences and cling to comfort. What we're trying to achieve is impossible, and what we're trying to escape from is inevitable. All our efforts to change things which can't be changed are futile, doomed to failure. In making all these efforts, we're out of step with the basic facts of life, jarring with reality – and it hurts.

We might think we know the facts of life ('Of course I'm going to die, that's obvious'), but knowing them on an intellectual level and accepting them in our hearts are two different things – we resist these truths with our emotions and our behaviour. Witness the explosion of cosmetic surgery in our culture – more than 34,000 invasive procedures a year in the UK; over 12 million such procedures carried out in the US each year.[2] Yet none of these expensive treatments will help us live longer, and they can only ever delay or mask the process of ageing. We may die wrinkle-free, with our faces fixed in a state of youthful paralysis, but will we really be any happier? The more we try to deny reality, the more suffering we experience. But we just keep on struggling anyway – raging at life's insults, trying to run away from them or taking elaborate steps to pretend they aren't happening. We are like animals trapped in a cage.

Fortunately, there's good news – the third noble truth states that there is a release from our predicament, and it comes in the form of the fourth truth, known as the eightfold path. This path is a programme of training, designed to help us come into step with reality and move with the flow of life, rather than against it. This is to be found in a different way of seeing, and a different way of being. To use the Buddha's analogy, we may have no choice about getting hit with the first arrow, but we can learn how to respond wisely to the distress it causes – we can learn not to fire the second arrow. Transformation of our experience is possible by discovering how to relate to it differently.

The path, as it was laid out 2,500 years ago, consists of eight elements: right understanding, right thought, right speech, right action, right livelihood, right exertion, right concentration, and right mindfulness. With right understanding and right thought, we come to accept the truth that things are impermanent, always changing; rather than railing against seemingly awkward realities, we can instead learn to appreciate, ride with and even celebrate the constant fluctuations in life. We might be able to appreciate the changing of the seasons – enjoying the delights of autumn and winter, rather than always wishing it were spring or summer. We can start to see that we're not fixed entities in isolation, but part of a flowing dynamic of interconnection with all things – with this view in mind, change becomes less of a threat and more of an opportunity.

As we develop this view, we can also cultivate the right speech, right action, right livelihood and right exertion that acknowledges, incorporates and works skilfully with these realizations. We can develop an attitude of compassion to others: we see that if we are interconnected, then everyone else's welfare is inextricably bound up with our own. We see that, by helping others, we can help ourselves.

RIGHT MINDFULNESS
But there's still something of a problem. If our minds remain distracted and speedy, we're likely to find that we often think, speak and act hastily, perhaps before we've

even noticed what we're really doing. If we aren't able to cultivate right concentration and mindfulness,[3] how can we practise any of the other parts of the path? Without some sense of calm in our minds, we'll continually be drawn into impulsive, unconscious activity – spinning around helplessly in old patterns of thinking, feeling and behaviour, even as we're trying to let go of them.

In traditional Buddhist descriptions, the distracted mind is like a wild animal. Sometimes the description is of a monkey, chattering away and throwing itself crazily all over the place, and at others times it's a rampaging elephant, ploughing heedlessly through the jungle, leaving devastation in its wake. If our mind is like this – frantic and untamed, or heavy and heedless, it's unlikely to listen to our command. However, it's said that, with practice, our minds will settle and we can develop stability, clarity and strength – mental qualities that can help us relate with life more effectively.

THE FOUR FOUNDATIONS OF MINDFULNESS

So how can the mind be trained to develop these qualities? The Buddha's suggestions were straightforward, and laid out in a teaching called The Four Foundations of Mindfulness. These instructions are considered to be especially important – the discourse begins by saying that: 'This is the direct way for the purification of beings, for the overcoming of sorrow and lamentations, for the end of suffering and grief, [and] for the attainment of the true way.'[4]

In the Four Foundations of Mindfulness, the Buddha describes four areas, or spheres, to which we can bring awareness. These four foundations relate to the body, the mind, feelings and to all the other phenomena that make up our life experience. However, before exploring each of these areas in detail, he first invites us to pay *particular* attention to our pattern of breathing – this practice is viewed as the ground from which we can cultivate all four foundations.

To practise mindfulness of breathing, it's suggested that we go somewhere quiet ('the forest, the foot of a tree, or an empty place') and sit down with our 'legs crossed, body erect, and mindfulness alert'. Being 'ever mindful', the meditation practitioner 'breathes in, [and] mindful, he breathes out. Breathing in a long breath, he knows, "I am breathing in a long breath." Breathing out a long breath, he knows, "I am breathing out a long breath."'

It's a simple invitation, perhaps deceptively so. We bring awareness to our breathing, so that when we breathe, we really know what we're doing – not just intellectually, but with the entirety of our being, a bit like we did at the start of the chapter. We breathe in deeply and, as we do so, place our full attention on what happens – we feel the sensation of air in our nostrils, the rising of our chest and the expansion of our abdomen. We know that we are 'breathing in a long breath'. Then, once we have inhaled fully, we mindfully breathe out, placing our attention on the movement of the breath as it leaves our body. We know that we are breathing out a long breath.

The description continues with an explanation of how the same attention is applied when the student's breathing is shallower: 'Breathing in a short breath, he knows, "I am breathing in a short breath." Breathing out a short breath, he knows: "I am breathing out a short breath."' Long or short, we simply relate with our breathing as it is – we don't need to try to change it or manipulate it in any way.

Next, there are suggestions for being mindful of our bodies. These include reminders on physical posture (the student 'knows, when he is standing "I am standing"... he knows, when he is lying down, "I am lying down"'), and performing daily activities ('in bending and stretching, he applies clear comprehension, in eating, drinking, chewing and savouring, he applies clear comprehension... in walking, in standing, in sitting, in falling asleep, in waking, in speaking and in keeping silence, he applies clear comprehension.'). As we go about our business (rather than our busyness) we can practise being aware of what we're doing, living consciously and wakefully.

Now the discourse turns to the other three foundations of mindfulness – making the same point with regard to each. So, the suggestions apply to the mind: the student 'knows the distracted state of consciousness as the distracted state of consciousness... the concentrated state of consciousness as the concentrated state' and to feelings: a student, 'when experiencing a pleasant feeling, knows, "I experience a pleasant feeling"; when experiencing a painful feeling, he knows, "I experience a painful feeling."' Note that we don't have to get rid of distractions, or try to create pleasant feelings – we just notice whatever's there, unbiased, without judgement.

The same applies to how we relate with every other aspect of our lives – when we're doing our jobs, perhaps, enjoying time with our friends and family, going shopping or even watching television, we are encouraged to look at what's going on. We're invited to notice how we experience the Four Noble Truths for ourselves – how we suffer and how clinging exacerbates our stress. And perhaps because so many of us have a tendency to get caught up in difficult experiences, we're reminded also to take notice when life is pleasant – to appreciate when we experience energy, joy, tranquillity, concentration and equanimity. And, in case we haven't yet got the message, we're even invited to take notice of our mindfulness – to be mindful of how mindful we are being.

The descriptions are simple and clear. If we want to suffer less, we can start by paying attention to our experience, rather than being so tied up in it, or trying to resist it. We can begin to observe life at the same time as participating in it – to really know what we're doing, as we're doing it. By watching what's happening in this way, we can begin to get a better sense of how we operate in the world, and become more alert to when our thoughts, emotions and behaviours create problems. We can start to get a better insight into what makes for a genuinely contented life. Rather than busily and mindlessly rushing through our lives, we can train in becoming more aware – we can wake up. If you'd like to continue this training yourself, we've included some more instructions on how to practise mindful breathing at the end of this chapter, on page 55.

This act of paying attention teaches us to rest with what's happening instead of just automatically reacting to it. Mindfulness creates a gap between impulse and action, a space in which we can notice our reactive tendencies without having to fall into them. While our mind will inevitably keep wandering off, we can train it to come back to awareness more often, just as we can train a puppy to sit still sometimes. As our mind's ability to stay focused grows, we can reside in this gap more often, and develop a greater capacity for choosing consciously how we behave. Through practising right concentration and mindfulness, we have more freedom to settle on right action, right livelihood, right speech and so on.

In this sense, training the mind in meditation is like training the body in physical exercise. Exertion is required to sit down and practise, and we have to make an effort to bring our mind to the breath, and to keep bringing it back when it wanders. It helps develop our power of attention in the same way that working out can help us develop our physical muscles – with practice, our minds can become stronger and more supple.

But meditation is also different from other forms of training, in that while there is effort required, we aren't striving for something to happen – our task, instead, is simply to bring our attention to how things are in the moment. This may seem like a paradox – how can we both make an effort, and let things be as they are? It all sounds rather different from how we might usually undertake a training programme, where there's a specific goal to aim for, and we think we won't get there unless we work really hard.

In meditation, we're not *trying* to relax – the Buddha's instructions on mindfulness of breathing apply as much to 'breathing in a short breath' as to 'breathing in a long breath'. If our breath is tense or shallow, we don't have to try and change that – we can simply be aware of that tension. Meditation may help relieve our stress, but it probably won't if we strive for it, just as struggling to go to sleep at night is a surefire way to prevent it happening. We can create the conditions for a good night's sleep – a comfortable bed, a quiet room, closing the curtains – but we can't drag ourselves into slumber. We can only let go into it, if it has the good grace to approach. Similarly, in meditation we can make the effort to sit down and follow the instructions, but we can't force the result we want.

The message here is that we can approach meditation with gentleness. We don't have to yank our attention back when it wanders – we can do so with kindness. This subtle balance between effort and letting go is one of the reasons the path of meditation is sometimes referred to as the 'middle way'. Walking this path does require a kind of discipline, but the suggestion is that, fundamentally, we don't need to try to change anything about ourselves – we're OK as we are. The curious thing is that if we can drop the struggle for a change and simply pay attention, a deep and unexpected kind of wellbeing often seems to emerge, revealing itself through its own natural process of unfolding.

TESSA'S EXPERIENCE

Tessa has been practising mindfulness meditation for 19 years – it has helped her to deal with stress and eczema, as well as giving her the ability to really appreciate life.

Tessa first became interested in meditation in 1992, when she was going through a particularly tough time at work. 'I was a trainee radio producer,' she remembers, 'working on a live daily programme. I was learning the ropes so I was quite stressed out. I had always suffered from eczema, but it was really bad at that point – my skin was red, inflamed, and itchy.'

Having booked herself a holiday in Corsica, Tessa spotted a book on meditation at the airport. Wondering if it might help with her stress, she took it away with her. 'I sat under a fig tree in the shade, and started to follow the instructions. I was looking for some sort of calm and peacefulness, and it gave me a glimpse of that.'

Back home, she started to look at how she might develop her practice further. 'I was invited by a friend to a local meditation centre – a Buddhist centre with a tradition of presenting meditation as something that anyone can do.'

Although at first Tessa was just looking for stress relief, she discovered something more. 'After a while, I did a full weekend of meditation, and that was when it really clicked for me. I discovered that the practice had something very profound to it, which I'd describe as an experience of much greater spaciousness, of the world being really vivid. I felt like I was stepping outside of the thought patterns that were trapping me, and feeling like there was a much bigger world out there.'

Although initially wary of anything that seemed too religious, Tessa began to take an interest in the origins of the practices she was being taught. 'I began to trust the Buddhist tradition, because everything that I was being told resonated with what I was discovering for myself. That encouraged me to investigate more, and slowly I became more interested in the kind of perspective it offers. It felt like something that could transform me as a person, although at the same time I was also settling into an acceptance of who I was, and not having to struggle so much to be something different.'

Tessa attributes many of the positive changes she has experienced over the years to her meditation practice. 'I am quite a speedy person, and before I started meditating I missed 99 per cent of what was happening in my day. I didn't even taste the food I was eating. I can be very caught up in all kinds of busy-ness, but through the practice we learn to let go of our thoughts and the habitual patterns that we are so addicted to. We are training in watching our mind and seeing how busy it is, and then dropping that. Because I'm practising, I'm much more able to notice when I'm walking down a street and there's a lovely tree in front of me. I can wake up to where I am in the present moment and really appreciate what's going on. I'm less trapped in thoughts about the past, or worries about the future. I feel more alive and awake to my own experience, and more accepting of it, rather than wishing things were different. That brings a sense of joy.'

Tessa also says that meditation has enabled her to respond more attentively when she is under pressure. 'I'm less reactive – I don't throw a temper tantrum or lash out at people as much as I used to. There are certainly still times when I feel my temper, but I'm more able to feel the thoughts and emotions that might be whirring around and causing me to react, and then be able to make a choice about the way I deal with that. I might still feel stress, but I don't buy into it as much. There's a sense of it happening in a bigger space, of not believing in it so strongly and of just observing it. I'm less likely to accelerate the stress by adding to it myself.' Meditation also seems to have had a tangible impact on Tessa's eczema. 'The difference is really noticeable – it's hardly there any more. It's gone from being a really difficult physical challenge to being very mild and under control.'

Over the years, Tessa has noticed how her degree of mindfulness seems to relate directly to how much she practises meditation. 'I've had periods where I have practised very regularly, and periods where I haven't,' she says, 'and I can always really feel the difference. When I'm practising for 10, 20 or 30 minutes in the morning, that seems to have a huge impact on whether I'm able to be more mindful during the rest of the day.'

You don't have to identify as a Buddhist to practise mindfulness, or to benefit from it. Mindfulness is certainly deeply rooted in Buddhism, but it doesn't belong to it exclusively – there are teachings designed to cultivate mindfulness in many of the world's great wisdom traditions. Ultimately, mindfulness is not Buddhist, Christian, Jewish, Muslim or atheist – it is a human quality that can be nurtured in anyone who chooses to practise it. All you need is the curiosity and courage to bring awareness to your inner world of thoughts, emotions and bodily sensations, as well as to the external aspects of your life, the situations you find yourself in and the people you relate to. Mindfulness comes from the willingness to investigate with interest every aspect of being alive, starting with one of the most basic of all experiences – your breath.

WHY PAY ATTENTION TO THE BREATH?
The Breath Is Fundamental to Our 'Being'

When we pay attention to the breath, we're engaging with life on its most essential level – awareness of our breathing shifts us naturally towards a deep experience of being. Paying attention to our breath, the very rhythm of existence, is a simple way to appreciate the magic of being alive.

Our Breath Is Always Available

If we are alive, we're breathing. By training to be mindful of the breath, we're becoming familiar with a simple tool that can always be used as a steadying anchor to bring us into awareness, wherever we happen to be.

We Don't Need to Control the Breath

That our breathing occurs without us having to do anything reminds us that underneath everything, sometimes we can just be – we don't always need to be chasing goals, forcing our experience or constantly analysing. We can let the breath breathe itself, and we can allow our present experience to be as it is, too. Paying attention to the breath reminds us that, in our hearts, we already know how to be.

THE BUDDHA AND PSYCHOLOGY

If what the Buddha said about mindfulness is true, then it was inevitable that his insights and methods would be discovered, corroborated and recommended by others, in different times, cultures and contexts. We've already seen how great philosophers through the centuries have praised the virtues of a mindful life – and now this has also started to happen in another field of exploration and study: the discipline of Western psychology.

With its focus on experimental methods to discover the truth about the human mind, Western psychology has much in common with Buddhism. The Buddha invited his followers to examine his teachings as if they were scientists testing a hypothesis. Using meditation, they could observe the effects of putting his suggestions into practice – they could watch their own minds in an interested, dispassionate way, like a researcher examining the results of an experiment.

For its part, Western psychology has long since appreciated the value of mindfulness in the quest for human happiness. William James, one of the founding fathers of the tradition, could have been talking about mindfulness when he wrote that 'the faculty of voluntarily bringing back a wandering attention, over and over again, is the very root of judgement, character and will. No one is master of himself if he have it not.'[5] Unfortunately, James was less confident about how this faculty might be developed, lamenting that 'it is easier to define this ideal than to give practical directions for bringing it about'.

Sigmund Freud was also onto something mindful when he recommended that psychoanalysts keep a 'calm, quiet attentiveness [and] evenly hovering attention' when they were seeing patients. Like the Buddha, Freud suggested that our present reality is affected by patterns of perceiving and behaving that have been set in the past, and he too suggested that the way to live more skilfully is to bring those patterns to consciousness. Freud's contemporary, Carl Jung, put this poetically: 'Your vision will become clear only when you look into your heart... He who looks outside, dreams. He who looks inside, awakens.'[6]

As Western psychology blossomed during the 20th century, more of its great practitioners had ideas which bear similarities to Buddhist teachings. In the 1950s, Albert Ellis suggested that mental illnesses such as depression arise not so much because of what happens to us, as how we interpret those events in our minds. Realizing that if you could change the way someone thinks, you might then relieve some of their emotional distress, Ellis developed a new form of treatment called 'Rational Emotive Behaviour Therapy'.[7] With its intention to relieve suffering by teaching people to relate differently with their experience, the framework behind Ellis' method (and that of cognitive behavioural therapy – a similar, currently popular approach) sounds not so different from the Four Noble Truths. Long before the advent of any of these therapies, the Buddha said that 'with our thoughts we make the world.'[8]

However, there's a missing link between the methods taught in Buddhism and those of Western psychologists in the first half of the 20th century. James, Freud and Ellis understood the importance of attention to the inner life, but their focus was primarily on analytical thinking as the catalyst for understanding and change. And while the cognitive behavioural tradition recognizes the important connections between thought, emotions and behaviour, by attempting to alter the content of our thoughts it can sometimes set people up for a subtle form of self-aggression – battling for change, rather than starting from a point of acceptance.

The missing link is meditation, which doesn't require analytical or positive thinking. Whether our experience is pleasant or unpleasant, positive or negative, in meditation we simply attend to it, with gentleness. It turns out that this act in itself is healing – it seems that shining the warm light of awareness on our habitual patterns starts to melt them in the same way that the sun might melt a block of ice. Similarly, when we stop giving energy to our old patterns, and instead just notice them, we may find they start to settle of their own accord, just as muddy water becomes clear when we stop stirring it.

The power of meditation practice came to the attention of Western psychology in the second half of the 20th century. This was the era when mindfulness really began to permeate our culture for the first time. Not only were some intrepid Westerners inspired to make the journey to Asia and learn these previously foreign ways, but some Asian teachers were coming the other way, to America and Europe. In the counter-culture of the 1960s and 1970s, these meditation masters found fertile ground for what they had to offer. Some educated but disaffected young people were eager to embrace new ways of living after the wartime suffering of previous decades. To many of them, Eastern philosophy and practices seemed to make more sense than some of their own inherited values.

Hippie endorsement meant that meditation became easily associated with flakiness, drugs and far-out spirituality. Nevertheless, the experience of the practice stayed with many of those who explored it, as did the benefits. Over time, some began to wonder if what they'd learned might be helpful to others – not just to seekers of enlightenment, but to ordinary men and women mired in everyday suffering.

If this was the case, wouldn't it make sense to present meditation in a way that would free it from the baggage of new-age philosophies? Mightn't this then appeal to people who would normally have been put off by otherworldly notions of nirvana, or other foreign-sounding ideas? If meditation really could relieve suffering, then wouldn't the validity of the teachings hold true when presented and tested in a different context – as psychology, perhaps, rather than religion? And if it were true, wouldn't this psychology be verifiable through the sophisticated experimental methods developed by modern science?

Some of these Western students of meditation became scientists or psychologists themselves, and a few not only pondered these questions but set themselves to answering them. Their work, as we shall see, has transformed how mindfulness is being presented in today's world.

PRACTICE: *Mindfulness of Breathing*

Before we move on to the next chapter, we'd like to
invite you to return to the practice of mindful breathing,
and to familiarize yourself with it a little more. As it can
be difficult to practise from written instructions alone,
we've also recorded guided audios leading you through
this and all the other practices in *The Mindful Manifesto* –
available to order or download from our website at www.
themindfulmanifesto.com. There is also a list of further
resources at the back of this book, pointing to ways you
can connect with others and develop your practice further.

STEP ONE: BODY POSTURE

First, find a space where you're unlikely to be interrupted.
It's helpful to sit on something comfortable and firm, which
will support your body to stay upright. If you choose to sit
in a chair, it's good if you can sit with your legs uncrossed,
your feet on the floor and your spine straight (although not
rigidly so) and away from the back of the chair, so it's self-
supporting. Or you can sit cross-legged on the floor, with
cushions to support your bottom – a couple of very large
books under the cushions can help provide a firm, steady
base. Lift your hands up onto your thighs, and rest them
there (one on either side of your lap) with the palms facing
down. You can close your eyes, or if you'd prefer to keep
them open, direct your gaze approximately 5 feet in front
of you, towards the ground – keeping your gaze soft, not
focusing on anything in particular. The posture is one of
confidence, openness and dignity – sitting a bit like a king
or queen on a throne.

STEP TWO: BREATH AWARENESS

Allow your breathing to settle – there's no need to try to breathe deeply or manipulate the breath in any way – just let your body breathe for you. Now, place your attention gently on the movement of the breath, sensing the cool air entering in through the nostrils, the filling of the abdomen, the rising and falling of the chest. Pay attention to the out-breath in the same way, noticing sensations as the breath is released from your body. Be aware of the body breathing in, and the body breathing out – inhaling and exhaling. Perhaps have a sense that your mind is riding the breath, a bit like you might ride a horse – synchronizing with it, feeling it, kindly and steadily. There's no need to concentrate hard – your attention can be precise but also light. You are not particularly trying to relax. Just allow yourself to be with your breathing, and your experience, however it is.

STEP THREE: WORKING WITH WHAT ARISES

As you continue to pay attention to your breathing, you may notice thoughts, feelings and bodily sensations arise. This is normal – thinking and feeling are part of being alive. However, while you are meditating, see if you can allow those thoughts, feelings and bodily sensations just to be there in the field of your awareness, without either holding on to them or shutting them out. Just acknowledge them, and let them go, as you continue to place the primary focus of your attention on your breath.

Before long, you will probably notice that your attention has wandered away from the breath. Perhaps your mind has started planning what you're going to have for dinner, or replaying a conversation you had earlier in the day. When you notice your attention has wandered, first acknowledge that (perhaps saying silently to yourself 'thinking' or 'mind wandering' if that helps), and then bring it gently back to the breath. As best you can, do this without any judgement or criticism – wandering is simply what the mind does – it's not a problem or a mistake. Just escort the mind gently back to the breath, as it moves naturally, in and out.

Soon, your mind will wander again – once more, just acknowledge that, and then return your attention to the breath, as it is, in the moment. Keep repeating this process – resting your attention on the breath and, when the mind wanders, patiently coming back to it. Continue with this for the period of time you have decided to meditate.

MINDFULNESS OF BREATHING: SUGGESTIONS FOR GETTING STARTED

SCHEDULING PRACTICE

Some people are better able to meditate in the morning, when their minds are fresh. Others prefer the evening, when they are more able to relax and let go of the day's pressures. Experiment with what works best for you. Whatever you decide, see if you can make your practice a habit, a bit like brushing your teeth. Remember that mindfulness is like any other skill – we get better at it the more we do it, and making time for periods of formal meditation is the way to train.

TIMING SESSIONS

Setting an alarm clock at the start of your practice makes a clear intention for how long you're going to meditate, and means your mind can let go of thinking about how much time is left before you stop.

PACING YOURSELF

Short, regular sessions tend to be the best way to start, rather than longer or more infrequent ones. It's better to sit for five or ten minutes than plan to meditate for an hour but never get around to it because it's too daunting or because you feel you don't have enough time. Developing a practice is a bit like starting physical exercise – you wouldn't try to complete a marathon before training your body with regular, shorter runs.

DON'T WAIT FOR CONDITIONS TO BE PERFECT

It's helpful to have a quiet place to meditate, and to feel ready and motivated before you begin. But if there are distractions, then, as best you can, just notice and accept them as you would notice your thoughts. Even if you don't feel in the mood to start, see if you can just do it anyway.

DROPPING PRECONCEPTIONS

'Meditation is religious… meditation is done by hippies or new-age weirdos… meditation is too hard for me… I'm too stressed out to meditate… I'm going to love meditating.' Whatever ideas and preconceptions you might have, see if you can let them go and approach the practice with what's sometimes called a 'beginner's mind' – with curiosity, and without prejudging what might happen.

STAYING WITH IT

Our overactive minds love having new toys to play with – including mindfulness practices. If we try lots of different techniques at once, we run the risk of using meditation as yet another way to keep our minds busy. Rather than racing ahead to the exercises in later chapters, or giving up after one session, see if you can practise mindful breathing every day, for ten minutes a day, until you feel familiar with it. Don't expect instant results – some meditators fruitfully work with just mindfulness of breathing for their whole lives.

WHAT IF I 'CAN'T' MEDITATE?

Lots of people sit down to meditate and find it difficult to pay attention to the breath. Distracted by the number or content of thoughts running through their mind, or feelings of anger, boredom or fear, they think they aren't capable of meditating – they aren't doing it properly, or are congenitally unsuited to the practice. Many of us play host to an internal slave-driver – we drag ourselves through the chores of the day and berate ourselves when we aren't 'good enough' at them. When this internal slave-driver meets meditation, it might tell us we're useless at it – especially if we haven't achieved complete calm and equanimity within the first few minutes. That's OK – it's just another habit our minds get into, perhaps built up over a long period of time, and it's part of what we work with in our practice.

In meditation, we are cultivating an attitude of self-compassion. So if you find you are giving yourself a hard time when you practise, just notice that, bringing a friendly awareness to it. Remember that there is no 'right' experience to have – meditation is a process of relating with whatever comes up, even if that's difficult – our task is simply to be aware of it, and keep on bringing our attention back to the object of our focus, which in this case is the breath. The thought 'I can't meditate' is just another judgement to relate with kindly. 'Oh, isn't that interesting?' you might say to yourself. 'I'm beating myself up for thinking I'm a bad meditator.' And then just return your attention to the breath, perhaps congratulating yourself for having noticed the judgement you were making. Even if you need to return your mind to the breath thousands of times, the practice is just to keep on doing so, as gently and patiently as you are able. This *is* meditation.

If you continue to struggle, it may help you to work with a meditation teacher (indeed, this can be very helpful for all of us as we continue along the path of mindfulness). There are some suggestions as to how you can find someone to work with in the Further Resources section on page 215).

Jonty's Experience

I wish I could say that I meditated every day. Unfortunately, like so many aspirations I have, what I know in theory is hard to translate into practice. Being mindful of my breathing is so simple, and I am aware that the effects on my life can be profound. Yet somehow I still struggle with it – as with many other things in my life, I tend to look for quick results, and when they aren't forthcoming, I get disappointed.

For a long time I imagined that I was just busier than everybody else, or that my mind was harder to work with than most. I used to look at other people as they sat and meditated and imagine their clear, tranquil minds, while inside mine it felt like a storm was raging.

Thankfully, much of the training I was given involved discussion groups where we could share our experiences, and during these I started to realize that I wasn't alone – other people were having similar difficulties, with physical aches and pains and wild minds that sometimes felt like they would never settle. Learning about meditation and mindfulness in a structured way like this was incredibly helpful. Sharing my experience with others gave me confidence and support.

As time has gone on I've started to notice my breath more often, and now I quite naturally place my mind on it when I want to relax. As soon as I do this, I become aware of my busy head, with all the thoughts bouncing around – energized by whatever emotion happens to be driving them at that moment. Within a few seconds I am usually carried off by them and have to remind myself, once again, to come back to my breath.

The stronger the emotion, the harder it is to let go, and I will often go back to the same thoughts again and again – reliving an argument, finding flaws in another person's case and strengthening my own, or daydreaming of escape from my current situation, perhaps planning my next holiday. Through all this my breath acts as an anchor. Sometimes when my mind is particularly stormy, it feels as though it won't hold and I fall back on all my usual techniques for managing anxiety by getting busy. With practice, though, my confidence in my breath, body and mind has grown and I know now that, at some level, I can work with any situation without drowning.

. . . .

Ed's Experience

My mind has always had a tendency to move fast. Sometimes this has served me well – at school and university, my quick intellect got me good grades and praise from teachers. As a journalist, being able to turn my thoughts into words at high speed seemed a crucial part of doing my job well. But a fast-paced mind has drawbacks: sometimes I am too caught up in my thoughts to notice what's going on around me – I miss the experience of actually being in the moment, of really living life. When there's too much going on in my head, I start to feel overwhelmed – and rather than slowing down I tend to speed up even more, trying to find an intellectual solution to a problem that's often made worse by over-thinking.

Mindfulness meditation – taking the time and space to connect with experience – is a simple antidote to my speed. I won't pretend that it has eliminated my tendency to go too fast – it hasn't. But meditation has given me a glimpse of what it's like to balance 'doing' with 'being' – to relax into experience, rather than always trying to control it. Mindfulness is a literal breathing space – it gives me choices, where previously there seemed few.

I still feel a strong pull to deal with problems by trying to get rid of them quickly, rather than staying present to the situation and experiencing the feelings it evokes. When I am practising mindfulness, it can feel as if I'm doing precisely the opposite of what I 'should'. However, it's no longer a surprise to find that I start to feel better once I relinquish control and instead pay attention.

Buddhist teachings tell us that these patterns are built up over many lifetimes, and are not easily changed – whether that's true or not, I take it as permission to be less than perfect and just do my best. I don't have to get it all sorted today, this week, or maybe even in this lifetime. Probably I am still less mindful than some people who have never meditated, but I see it very much like physical exercise – we all start at different levels of fitness, and our minds, as well as our bodies, have different capacities. I may not always be mindful, but I am certainly more mindful than I used to be. That's good enough for now.

. . . .

CHAPTER 3

MINDFULNESS OF BODY

Practise listening to the wisdom of your body – coming into a mindful relationship with your physical form can bring deep healing.

Many of us have troubled relationships with our bodies. Perhaps we don't like the way they look – they're too tall, too small, too fat, too thin or too old. Or they don't behave the way we want – they give us pain, or don't work the way they used to. Sometimes we ignore our bodies, disregarding our health and then getting surprised when we become unwell. At other times we worship our bodies, creating a temple of them and religiously sticking to whatever diet plan or exercise that might promise to keep us fit.

Each of these approaches has something in common – none of them relates with the body as it is, with acceptance, compassion and care. Whether we're resisting, ignoring or obsessed with our bodies, we aren't at peace in our physical home. We objectify our form, which means we can't truly inhabit it. We become dissociated, caught in a stressful relationship with our body that's mainly managed through the discursive mind – how we think ourselves to be, rather than how we actually are. When we relate with ourselves in this conceptual way, our minds and bodies are separated at a distance. We feel divided, disembodied.

Because of this separation, we miss much of what our bodies have to tell us. They're constantly sending us signals, a steady stream of feedback on our lives. This feedback is sometimes described as intuition, having an inkling, a gut reaction or funny feeling. It may get dismissed as irrational, but there's nothing very strange about it – it's just information that tells us physically how we're doing. Our body acts like a physical barometer, reflecting the weather of our internal world. If we have an infection, our body lets us know with discomfort and fever; if we feel threatened, it lets us know through sweaty palms, dry mouth and stomach churning; and if we've been overexerting ourselves, the body lets us know through exhaustion, a call to rest. We now know that there are neural networks all over our bodies, sending electrical signals to our brain – whether we choose to listen or not, our body is communicating.

Many of us become aware of our body's signals only when we get really sick, stressed or tired – we aren't attuned to the more subtle sensations that are present all the time, and which we could use to guide our decision-making. This was demonstrated in an experiment conducted by the neurologist Antonio Damasio: he measured the electrical conductance of subjects' palms during a gambling task in which the cards were rigged, and found that people's bodies sensed the deception around five to eight times more quickly than their minds. Their hands started registering signs of nervousness (a higher level of conductance) when they were about to draw from a rigged deck, even though their conscious minds remained unaware of the fraud.[1]

We are less likely to notice cues from our bodies when we are stuck in our thoughts, rushing around like brains on sticks. We don't hear when our bodies tell us it's time to slow down, eat healthily or exercise. Is it any wonder, then, that medical practices and hospital clinics are flooded with patients reporting 'unexplained' aches, pains and fatigue?[2] When we don't listen to them, eventually our bodies protest in the only way they can, beckoning for attention with symptoms of dis-ease. They cry out for healing.

When we get sick, rather than treating our bodies with tenderness and care, we often just objectify them even more. We take them to the GP like we'd take a second-hand car to the garage, hoping to get them prodded and patched up for the road. We expect the doctor to ask a few questions, do some tests and try to fix us up. But many symptoms don't fit into neat categories – they can't be resolved by looking at an X-ray or having an operation. The common assumption that doctors can cure us is frequently false; many medical conditions are chronic, and we have to learn to live with them. Some 20 per cent of adults in the UK suffer from chronic pain[3] – and doctors can often do little to help them.

The lack of a medical solution can make things worse. We long to feel better, and so struggle to improve things. We fight for a cure – surely the doctor can order some more tests, or send us for a second opinion? There must be a tablet, an injection, a treatment programme that can make our bodies work well again – after all, if they can clone sheep, surely they must be able to get rid of my pain? Unfortunately, this desperate search for answers can lead to even greater stress. We get angry at our bodies, cruelly cajole them to operate in spite of our condition, or reject them, giving up on self-care. We fire the second arrow of suffering onto the first arrow of pain.

Modern medical practice doesn't always help matters. Doctors' training breeds a mechanical kind of health care – the human 'machine' is broken down into all of its material components, and the doctor's job is to try to work out where the problem is and then resolve it. Medicine has developed this way of working because it's based on scientific method, which relies on detailed observation and experimentation to find out how things work. In many respects it's a fine way of doing things – scientific detail has brought amazing advances in the treatment of many illnesses, especially over the last century. But it has its drawbacks, meaning we place far greater importance on what we can see than what we can't, focusing in on material detail rather than zooming out and taking in the bigger picture.

It's easy to lose sight of the fact that we're not just biology and chemistry. We are an interconnected matrix: of physical components, yes, but also our emotions, thoughts and relationships, everything that makes up our conscious experience and which so profoundly affects our wellbeing. Taken to its extreme, medical health care sometimes doesn't notice our minds at all – you still hear trainee doctors talking about 'the amazing heart murmur in bed 14' or 'the liver cancer in bed 22'. Patients become their diagnosis – a collection of disconnected flesh and bones.

Despite all our amazing technology, we don't have cures for many conditions that afflict us – heart disease, high blood pressure, asthma or arthritis. Medicine can help us manage these illnesses, but in most cases there's no way to get rid of them. Even with the best physicians, the best medicine and the best technology, our bodies still wear out – we will have to face ageing, sickness and death. If health care is just about fixing us up, it's doomed to failure. So might there be a more skilful way of working with our bodies, even when they aren't in good shape?

A DIFFERENT KIND OF HEALTH

It has been shown again and again in studies that our mood and thinking processes affect when and how we get sick, as well as our prospects for recovery. People prone to mental illness are at a much higher risk of a whole range of other health problems, including cardiovascular disease and diabetes.[4] Chronic stress itself is a major cause of illness[5] – it increases our blood pressure, making us more likely to suffer a heart attack or stroke, and weakens our immune systems so that we are more likely to get infections. It contributes to skin disorders such as eczema and psoriasis, and plays an important part in conditions like irritable bowel and chronic fatigue. It can also give us headaches and migraines, as well as disturbing our sleep – placing our bodies under even more strain.

To address this issue, we can't just ask the mechanic to fix our body/machine – we need to take a closer look at how we're driving. In the late 1970s, molecular biologist Jon Kabat-Zinn began teaching patients to do just that. At the time he was working in the cell biology and anatomy department at the University of Massachusetts Medical School. But his inspiration was moving in another direction. One of those young people who had made a powerful connection to the practice of meditation, Kabat-Zinn looked around at his work environment and saw suffering, the first noble truth, staring him in the face. Like all hospitals, it was full of sick people, and many of them had come to the end of the road with conventional medicine. When he asked his clinical colleagues what proportion of patients they could truly help, the figure that came back was depressing: maybe one in seven, one in ten. The rest either got well on their own or stayed sick.

Kabat-Zinn came up with an idea. What if he were to put together an intensive training in meditative disciplines – the kind that was taught in a Buddhist monastery or retreat centre – and offer it right there in the hospital, to people the doctors had little to offer? What if he challenged them to work with their suffering in a new way? Of course, he realized that meditation wouldn't get rid of their pain, but could it help them relate with their very serious problems from a different perspective? Could they learn to uncouple the experience of discomfort from all their reactions to it – the storylines about how 'This is killing me,' and 'I can't stand it,' or 'Why can't the doctors make it go away?'

The response was enthusiastic – if Kabat-Zinn felt he could do something useful for these people, the hospital clinicians would be more than happy to send some his way. Many patients were so desperate they'd be willing to try anything their doctors recommended, no matter how weird it might sound. Meditation for cancer, heart disease, diabetes – sure, why not? There wasn't anything else left in the medical bag.

Kabat-Zinn called his programme Mindfulness-Based Stress Reduction (MBSR). Over eight weekly sessions, he taught groups of people a range of practices – mindful breathing, a 'body scan' meditation (in which attention is brought to different parts of the body in turn), and gentle movement exercises from the Hatha Yoga tradition. He also taught them how to cultivate awareness during activities such as eating and walking – to take what they were learning into their daily lives.

The course was no fluffy option – Kabat-Zinn knew the gravity of what many of these patients were facing, and he knew that what he calls 'dime-store relaxation techniques' wouldn't make much difference. As part of their homework in between sessions, participants were asked to practise meditation for 45 minutes a day for the duration of the course.

Although he had received his own mindfulness training in a Buddhist context, Kabat-Zinn knew that it wouldn't make sense to teach his patients as if they were Buddhists. Many wouldn't be interested in adopting a spiritual or moral path, and others might already have one of their own – in any case, such an approach would have seemed inappropriate for a health-care setting. There was no attempt to hide the origins of the practices, but there were no robes, shrines, chanting or other elements that might be easily construed as religious. As straightforwardly as possible, the course taught meditation as a way of working with suffering.

This secular approach is in tune with Buddhist teachings that warn of getting hung up on the trappings of belief. When Kabat-Zinn discussed with Zen master Morinaga Roshi how to teach mindfulness to people who might find Buddhism a barrier, his response was unequivocal: 'Throw out Buddha! Throw out Zen.'[6] There was no need to hold on to ways of teaching that prevented people from accessing the benefits of meditation. If the methods worked, they would help – as long as their essence was transmitted skilfully.

BEING IN OUR BODIES

There's nothing exclusively Eastern about bringing mindfulness to the body – its principles are inherent in our Western language of wellbeing, too. The words 'healing' and 'health' are closely connected to the notion of wholeness – healing in some sense means 'becoming complete'. Similarly, the word rehabilitation literally means 'to re-inhabit' – when we rehabilitate from an illness, we are coming to live again in our bodies. Mindfulness practice invites us to do this by reconnecting to our physical selves.

This healing actually comes from accepting and facing up to the difficulties and limitations of our bodies – experiencing them, even when that might not be pleasant. Learning how to notice our pain rather than being consumed by it, how to be with it rather than blocking it. Contrary to all our impulses, we let go of the attempt to be free of discomfort, and instead turn our attention inwards, coming closer to our experience and really seeing it, feeling it, being with it. We approach with awareness the very things we've been trying to avoid, as if to say, 'Hello, pain – I know you're here, and I accept you.'

This may sound counterintuitive, but it seems to help, as an experiment by Delia Cioffi and James Holloway at the University of Houston demonstrates.[7] Cioffi and Holloway wanted to examine the effects of three different ways of relating to pain: distracting from it, suppressing it, and monitoring it, the last of which we might call mindfulness. First they had 63 people dip their hands in ice-cold water. Then they asked some of their subjects to think about their bedroom at home (distraction), others to try not to think about the pain in their hands (suppression), and the rest to pay close attention to the sensations of discomfort (monitoring/mindfulness). Cioffi and Holloway found that the monitoring group recovered from the pain fastest, and those who tried to suppress the pain recovered most slowly. The pain-suppressors also seemed to become more sensitive to pain – they had a lower threshold for interpreting a simple vibration as painful when exposed to it later on.

PRACTICE: *The Ice Cube Experiment*

You could try a version of this experiment yourself. Take a few ice cubes from the freezer and place them in a cup or bowl. Find somewhere you can sit comfortably and spend a few moments practising mindful breathing. When you feel ready, take one of the ice cubes in your hand and gently close your fist – remembering that it's fine to open your hand and put the ice cube back at any time.

Now, bring your attention to the sensations in your hand. Rest your awareness on them, in the same way that we've been resting awareness on the breath. Notice the effect of ice in your palm – feel it, be curious about it. Does the sensation change over time, becoming more or less intense? Be interested in the quality of the experience. Notice also how you automatically react – do you want to stop the experiment because the ice is cold? Or perhaps there's a thought: 'I don't like it!' or 'I must be crazy trying this!' Or maybe a kind of bravado takes you over – 'Hah! It's just a bit of ice – call that pain? Bring it on!' Is it possible to separate these reactions from the actual experience of holding the ice? As best you can, each time your attention wanders away from the sensation, just gently bring it back, as you might when the mind wanders away from the breath in mindful breathing. If the ice melts completely before you decide to stop, perhaps try it again with another cube, and see if the experience is any different.[8]

PRACTICE: *Working with Discomfort*

You can try this practice with physical discomfort, too. The next time you feel pain, notice its location and then experiment with bringing your awareness to it, even if your instinct is to recoil. See if you can lean into your experience a little – move your mind towards it, approach it, come up close to it. Notice what kind of pain it is – a long, dull ache, perhaps, or a repeating, sharp kind of throb? Can you investigate the textures without getting caught up in what the pain means, or whether you like or dislike it? Is it solid and continuous, or does it subtly change, ebbing and flowing somewhat? Notice too any aversion to the pain – a thought of not wanting to pay attention to it, or of feeling hostile towards it, or of wanting it to stop – notice these reactions in as friendly and compassionate a way as you can. Investigate if there is any tension in your body along with the pain – perhaps in your shoulders, jaw or legs – and if there is, just allow that tension to drop if you're holding it consciously. But don't struggle to get rid of it; if it seems stuck, just accept it with as much compassion as you can.

If you like, experiment with a sense of breathing into the area of pain or tension. With each in-breath, visualize that the breath flows to that area of the body, and with each out-breath visualize that the air flows out from it, as if you are softly bathing the area of discomfort with attention. Or if that feels too overwhelming, bring your mind back to your breathing itself and allow the discomfort to exist more at the fringes of your awareness, letting it be, doing its thing, as you rest your mind on the breath, using it as an anchor to hold the experience. You could also try widening your attention so that it's holding the whole of your body, cradling it in awareness a bit like you might cradle a child – gently, kindly – perhaps noticing sensations of touch where your body meets the ground or the clothes you're wearing. Play with these ways of relating to the physical sensations in the body, knowing that it's fine to stop, take a break and make a fresh start at any time. Of course, you don't need to be in pain to try this practice – it's good to connect mindfully with our bodies at any time.

There's no right or wrong experience to have when you're practising with body sensations in this way. Whether you find it scary, boring, frustrating or enjoyable, the practice is simply to notice those reactions along with the body sensations themselves – to be with them, and accept them, just as they are.

Acceptance here is not the same as resignation – we aren't giving up on our bodies, and we can continue to follow whatever sensible steps are recommended to us by doctors. We may still take medication, have surgery or try some other form of therapy – if mindfulness can help us reduce our stress, it will give other treatments the best chance of working, and ourselves the best chance of recovery. Although mindfulness may not cure us in the conventional sense, it invites us to take care of ourselves, to investigate the possibility of transformation through a kinder, more attentive way of being. Even if our pain doesn't change, perhaps we can hold it in a less claustrophobic, less aggressive way?

An artificial split between mind and body has been perpetuated in our culture for a long time, and letting go of old habits isn't easy. Healing this division is an especially difficult task when we have a chronic illness and are in pain – exactly when we are most likely to want to shut off from our bodily experience. In these circumstances, directing awareness to what's most difficult sounds like masochism – after all, chronic physical illness is a bit different from holding an ice cube for a few minutes. Can we really be sure it's worth it?

Jon Kabat-Zinn's first students must have felt they had little choice. They'd exhausted all other options and came to him as a last resort. They had to take it on trust that practising mindfulness might help – to be willing to engage with it, taking a leap and seeing what might happen. For many of them, it seems to have been a leap worth taking. Patients who had previously felt defeated reported new hope, and a way of living more peacefully with themselves and their condition. Their progress was often amazing – after years of feeling disabled by illness, they began to accept their bodies, carving out new and fulfilling lives as they explored the edge of their limitations.

JULIE'S EXPERIENCE

Julie is 35 and has a serious inflammatory condition of the bowel called Crohn's disease, which she's had since she was a teenager. There's no cure, and, when it flares up, she's in a lot of pain.

Stress makes Julie's condition worse. 'With Crohn's disease you feel physically really unwell. I was working in a very tough job and I would drink Diet Coke or coffee to get through the day. I would come home and just collapse. In the end my health totally crashed and I was unable to continue working.'

Julie referred herself to a mindfulness course at King's College Hospital in London. She says that the meditation practices have helped her see the effect her reactions and lifestyle were having on her body. 'I clearly saw my thinking patterns for the first time and how they increased my anxiety and negative feelings about my illness. I was using my job as a way of avoiding having to deal with anxiety. I think that's the thing about meditation, combined with CBT [cognitive behavioural therapy] – it very gently helps you question some of your thinking. Mindfulness helped me separate my thinking from reality; I now make very different, more gentle choices about how I care for myself and spend my time. I know I never want to return to such a stressful environment.'

Mindfulness has also helped Julie learn to listen to her body a lot more. 'I had denied my Crohn's disease for a long time. Mindfulness practice has allowed me to accept my condition and recognize that I am physically quite ill. Ignoring what my body was trying to tell me was just damaging me further.'

From being in a place where her mind and body were not very connected, Julie now feels much more at peace with herself. 'I have gone from seeing it as this thing that I didn't want to deal with – an inconvenience – to it now being part of me. It's a much more accepting relationship. Rather than seeing it as a kind of hindrance – something to get annoyed with myself at – I can be more compassionate to myself, my body, and my situation.

'It has changed my life in such a positive way. My meditation practice has become an integral part of my day, my anxiety levels continue to lessen, and it has had a positive impact on my health, which I now try to deal with a day at a time.'

Stories from patients are heartening, but to have a chance of being adopted more widely in the medical world, the mindfulness-based stress-reduction programme needed more than just anecdotes. It had to stand up to scientific scrutiny through empirical testing, the same way that any other medical treatments are assessed. Indeed, perhaps it needed to pass these empirical tests even more than other methods, because what it appeared to offer seemed so 'alternative'. Could Kabat-Zinn show MBSR's effectiveness, not just in terms of patient reports, but in clinical trials – medicine's own gold standard of proof?

MBSR: THE SCIENCE

Because it has a simple, clear and easily replicable format, MBSR lends itself easily to this kind of research. Many patients can be put through the same training and, by evaluating how they respond, it's possible to discover whether the programme really helps.

The research started with a small trickle of studies carried out by Kabat-Zinn and his colleagues, but as news of the course spread, other clinicians and researchers began offering it to their patients and analysing the results. The outcomes have been similar all over the world – hundreds of papers have offered compelling evidence that MBSR does indeed reduce stress, help people deal with the symptoms of illness and improve their quality of life. In one early inner-city trial (in Meriden, Connecticut), participants' anxiety levels fell by 70 per cent after they took the course.[9] Their reported medical symptoms also reduced by 44 per cent, and they visited their doctor much less often.

The effects seem to be long-lasting, too – another early trial found that not only did participants get less anxious during and after the course, but most were still feeling the benefits three years later.[10] The MBSR programme also seems to help people enjoy a more harmonious relationship with their bodies.[11] In one of Kabat-Zinn's studies, participants were asked to rate how far they considered each part of their body to be problematic. At the end of the course, the scores had fallen by around 30 per cent, suggesting that these patients' minds and bodies were no longer in such a state of struggle.

As the quantity and quality of data has grown, researchers have begun to compile reviews and meta-analyses of the evidence – pooling them to come up with an overall picture of the programme's impact. These have consistently concluded that MBSR reduces stress and increases emotional wellbeing across a wide array of wellbeing measures (less anxiety, better mood, improved sleep, more vitality).[12] The programme has also shown a positive impact on people's ability to cope with a range of specific medical conditions, including diabetes, cancer, fibromyalgia, arthritis, multiple sclerosis, epilepsy, chronic fatigue, irritable bowel syndrome and heart disease.

HELPING WITH PAIN

And what about pain? Most of the people who came to the stress reduction clinic were reporting some kind of physical pain, which conventional medicine had not been able to alleviate. Even though MBSR makes no attempt to remove pain, by learning a different way of relating to it – experiencing it without judgement, rather than getting angry with it or trying to get rid of it – are participants able to interpret their pain in a different way, and be less troubled by it? It seems so. In some of the first research on the programme, patients reported feeling less pain at the end of the course compared to a control group, as well as being less restricted by their pain. And 65 per cent of patients who hadn't responded to standard medical treatments were less troubled by pain after taking part.[13] A follow-up study four years after the programme found that the gains experienced by patients had been maintained long term.[14]

More recent studies have also suggested that meditation practice has an effect on our ability to cope with pain. Researchers at the University of North Carolina have found that people who meditated for 20 minutes a day had higher pain thresholds after just four days – they were given small electric shocks, and those rated as 'high pain' before meditation diminished to 'low pain' afterwards.[15] Of course, the intensity of the shocks remained the same, so it was the subjects' relationship with the discomfort that changed. An experiment at Wake Forest University School of Medicine reported that another short training in meditation reduced pain's unpleasantness by 57 per cent, and subjects rated the same pain as 40 per cent less intense. This shift was mirrored in their brains, which were scanned using magnetic resonance imaging – brain activity decreased in areas known to process painful stimuli.[16]

WHAT'S HAPPENING IN THE BODY?

It seems clear that mindfulness helps people reduce their stress, as well as the intensity of their pain and suffering. But what's actually going on in their bodies? Can meditation transform not just how we relate to our bodies, but biology itself?

Some of the early research on meditation reported effects on the body's metabolism – in the 1970s, scientists Herbert Benson and Robert Wallace found it could lead to health-promoting changes in the body, including a lowering of blood pressure and heart rate.[17] However, the first studies to investigate the impact of mindfulness-based stress reduction on the body was carried out by Kabat-Zinn and a team of dermatologists. They studied a group of patients with psoriasis – a common skin condition which produces 'plaques' of thickened, red scaly skin on the body.[18] Psoriasis is made worse by stress, and it also seems likely that the body's immune system plays a part in its development. The immune system normally protects us from harm, but in patients with psoriasis, cells from this system build up in the skin, releasing chemicals that cause inflammation and an overgrowth of cells in the affected area.

Most treatments for psoriasis try to reduce the inflammation or dampen the immune system by slowing down cell growth. This is usually done with powerful creams applied to the plaques, but if the psoriasis is widespread, patients are sometimes given ultraviolet light treatment, known as phototherapy. Given that stress usually makes psoriasis worse, Jon Kabat-Zinn and his colleagues wanted to find out if practising mindfulness could have the opposite effect, and enhance the effect of phototherapy.

The researchers divided the patients into two groups, and while one set received their usual light treatment, the others were also guided through a set of mindfulness meditation techniques. Pictures were taken of the psoriasis before the treatment started, and again at regular intervals throughout the trial, until the plaques had disappeared. The results were striking: the skin of the patients who listened to the tape as well as receiving phototherapy cleared four times more quickly than those who just had the light treatment.

More evidence that mindfulness can affect the immune system came from a study of MBSR offered to office workers in Madison, Wisconsin. At the end of the course, the participants were given a flu vaccination, as were some of their colleagues who hadn't received the training. Vaccinations stimulate the immune system to produce antibodies to a virus, which are then able to recognize and destroy that virus if it gets into the body again. The stronger a person's immune system, the greater the antibody response to the vaccination. Earlier studies had shown that being under stress can lower antibody response, and the investigators wanted to see if taking the programme could increase it. A few weeks after the vaccination, the flu antibody level in the bloodstream of the workers who had been practising meditation showed, as predicted, a higher antibody response than those who hadn't taken the course.[19]

If mindfulness can help our immune systems handle illnesses like psoriasis and the flu, could it also help us manage more serious conditions, like cancer or HIV? Linda Witek-Janusek and her colleagues in Chicago offered an MBSR course to 38 women after they'd had surgery for breast cancer, and then compared their recovery to that of another 31 women.[20] Witek-Janusek found that the women who took the course had lower levels of the stress hormone cortisol, and that their immune systems recovered more quickly after treatment – they had a higher level of what is called 'natural killer cell activity'. Natural killer cells can recognize and destroy cancer cells – the more active they are, the better chance there is of being able to clear the cancer and prevent it from returning. Several other studies of MBSR with cancer patients have also found lower levels of cortisol and improved immune function.[21]

At the University of California, David Creswell examined the effects of MBSR on the immune systems of 48 people with HIV.[22] They measured the patients' level of CD4 T cells, which help coordinate the immune system when it has to respond to a threat. These are the cells that the HIV virus destroys, damaging the immune system and leaving people prone to infections and cancers that could otherwise be fought off easily. Creswell found that the level of CD4 T cells in participants who had been through the mindfulness programme remained constant during the course, compared to a control group whose CD4 T cell count dropped.

He also found that those participants who did the most mindfulness practice showed the greatest benefit to their immune systems. Another study of MBSR for patients with HIV found beneficial effects on the immune system, too, including increased natural killer cell activity and increased production of b-chemokines, which are molecules that prevent the HIV virus infecting healthy cells.[23]

Mindfulness practice also seems to affect the rate at which our cells age, a key factor in how long we live. The cells in our bodies all contain chromosomes – these are made up of strands of DNA, which are encoded with all the information the cell needs to reproduce. At the ends of the chromosomes is an area called the 'telomere' which protects the chromosome from damage. With every replication of a cell, these telomeres become slightly shorter and, eventually, once they are shortened to a certain length the cell will stop replicating. This is thought to be the biological process by which we age, and there's evidence it may be accelerated by stress.[24] The stress hormone cortisol affects the chemical balance in our cells, causing what is known as oxidative stress, and this is thought to damage telomerase, the enzyme in the cells which maintains telomere length. If telomerase cannot work, then there's nothing to stop the telomeres shortening, and we will age more quickly. Given that meditation seems to reduce stress, a team of scientists led by University of California at Davis researcher Tonya Jacobs decided to investigate whether it has any impact on telomerase.

To find out, Jacobs and her team measured telomerase activity in participants who had taken part in a three-month mindfulness retreat, and then compared them to a control group. They found that, as well as showing increases in sense of control and purpose in life, plus decreases in neuroticism, telomerase activity in the mindfulness group's white blood cells was a third higher than in the control group. The participants who showed the highest levels of telomerase were also those who showed the most improvement in measures of psychological wellbeing. Could it be that practising mindfulness leads to an increase in telomerase activity, which in turn helps slow the rate of cellular ageing, potentially helping us live longer? It's a hypothesis which needs further investigation, but the signs are very interesting.[25]

In each of these cases it seems that the body is responding favourably to a reduction in stress. Just as symptoms of illness can be exacerbated by tension, so the letting go of stress that can come with mindfulness training seems to help protect us from illness and gives our bodies a greater chance to heal – we experience the benefits not just as an attitude of mind, but in the very tissue and fibre of our physical make-up.

STRESS AND THE AUTONOMIC NERVOUS SYSTEM

Evolutionary history has primed us to react when our safety is threatened. Through our autonomic nervous system – which keeps our heart beating, our bowels moving and lungs breathing – we instinctively react when we sense danger, automatically getting ready to fight or run away. The autonomic nervous system releases adrenaline, diverting resources to parts of the body that might need to step up a gear – our heart rate increases and blood moves from our gut to our muscles. Cortisol is released, and this raises blood-sugar and blood-pressure levels, giving us a short-term energy boost that primes us to deal quickly with the crisis. When the danger seems to have passed, the body can relax again – blood pressure reduces, our heart rate slows and blood flows back to the stomach – making it easier for us to digest food again.

This 'fight or flight' response helped early humans survive – like most other animals, our ancestors had to react instantaneously to the movement of predators that wanted to kill them. But in a relatively short space of time – just a few thousand years – our lifestyles have changed. We now live in a 21st-century world of offices, cars and deadlines rather than caves, spears and predators. We still face physical threats – the danger of crossing a busy road, for example – but most of us, most of the time, experience stressors that are low-level and chronic: the constant demands placed on us by the world to pay bills, meet deadlines or reply to e-mails. Responding to these pressures doesn't really require the outpouring of adrenaline that was necessary to run from a sabre-toothed tiger. Nevertheless, conditioned as we are by millions of years of evolution, we still react to these pressures as though we are in grave physical danger – our autonomic nervous system keeps us on red alert.

This is how stress contributes to physical ill-health. When we get no relief from the threat to our wellbeing – whether it's a chronic illness or the pressure of living an overloaded life – our bodies don't come back into balance. Our autonomic nervous system gets stuck on overdrive, and we feel tense all the time. The 'fight or flight' reaction, which was meant to give us a short-term boost in a crisis, puts our bodies under constant duress. Our pulse stays fast and blood pressure remains high, increasing the risk of a stroke or heart attack. The immune system is dampened, making us more prone to infections, and possibly even cancer. By predisposing us to illness and putting extra strain on our bodies, long-term stress can speed up ageing and shorten our lives.[26]

Whatever the issue that's triggering our tension, if we keep feeling stressed, the problem will likely get worse. However, scientific research on the MBSR programme seems to be showing that we can start to regulate the autonomic nervous system more consciously – taking charge of how our bodies respond to threats. Through meditation practice, we can become less fearful, releasing ourselves from the grip of 'fight or flight' as the only possible responses to difficulties in life. We can notice our tendency to react automatically, resist habitual impulses and increase our ability to choose what to do. This in turn allows our bodies to calm down from a state of heightened alert, leading to lower levels of cortisol, higher levels of telomerase and a stronger immune system.

A FRUITFUL DIALOGUE

The approach to chronic illness offered by MBSR is both ancient and revolutionary. It presents the wisdom of meditation practice in a way that connects with people who might not otherwise be interested, and in a way that can be tested scientifically. By putting the programme under the microscope, medicine and meditation have come to engage in a fruitful dialogue. Scientific data may not reflect the deep learning which comes from those 'Aha' moments when new practitioners realize that they can be friendly to their bodies, even when they are in pain – but it can and does provide important evidence for what they describe.

Thirty years after Jon Kabat-Zinn started offering mindfulness training to hospital patients, more than 19,000 people have taken the stress reduction course at what has grown into the Center for Mindfulness in Medicine, Health Care, and Society at the University of Massachusetts Medical School. And there are now hundreds, possibly thousands of similar programmes running in clinics across the globe.

A PARADIGM SHIFT

Mindfulness training represents the possibility of a paradigm shift in how we approach our health. When we treat our bodies as machines to be taken to the garage for servicing and repairs, we disempower ourselves – handing over the keys for our wellbeing to 'experts'. Of course, it's sensible to use the wonderful technologies of modern medicine to help when they can – they often bring healing that we could only dream of a few decades ago. But by also learning practices that can help us heal from the inside, we can start to become more skilled in looking after our own bodies.

When people come to mindfulness training, they often realize at a gut level the importance of this integrated approach to health care. Perhaps this is partly why the MBSR programme is such a popular approach – around 85 per cent of participants complete the course, and around three-quarters are still practising some of the meditations up to four years later.[27]

We don't need to wait for our bodies to protest in order to start hearing what they're telling us – everyone can benefit from practising mindfulness. By bringing attention into the body, synchronizing it with our mind, we can tune in more easily to its messages. We can do this based not just on what we're told is good for us, but by listening to the wisdom that already lies within, and which reveals itself through meditation.

PRACTICE: *Mindfulness of Body*

In this practice, sometimes known as a body scan, we take awareness to each part of our body in turn. It's good to practise this with either a live instructor or guided audio – however, if you are practising unguided, we suggest you allow between 20 and 45 minutes.

STEP ONE
Find a place where you can lie down comfortably on a rug, soft carpet or bed. Cover yourself with a blanket if it helps you keep warm. Close your eyes, and allow your body to let go into the ground that's supporting it – feel your body being held from beneath, perhaps noticing points where the body makes contact with the floor, bed or rug.

STEP TWO

Practise mindfulness of breathing for a while, settling your attention on the movement of the breath in the lower abdomen.

STEP THREE

Direct your attention down your left leg, into your left foot and to your left big toe. Notice any sensations present there – any warmth or coolness, tingling or pulsing, contact with your clothing or the air around. This doesn't mean thinking about the toe, so much as experiencing it directly. Rest your attention on the toe, registering what's going on in this part of the body.

STEP FOUR

When the mind wanders away from the toe – perhaps following a thought, or drawn to what's going on in another part of the body, acknowledge where the mind has gone, and gently escort your attention back to the toe. Remember that mind-wandering isn't a failure or a problem; it's just what minds do. See if you can cultivate an attitude of friendliness and compassion to yourself as you practise.

STEP FIVE

Take your attention now to the other toes of the left foot, resting your mind on each for a few moments, and returning attention to them when the mind wanders. Next, expand your awareness to the whole of the left foot, investigating each area with a sense of curiosity and interest. If you notice yourself making judgements about your experience (such as liking the practice, or finding it irritating), acknowledge those judgements, without attaching to them or trying to push them away – and come back to awareness of the foot.

STEP SIX
Continue to scan the rest of the body in the same way, taking your attention to each part in turn. Bring awareness to the left leg – the ankle, shin and calf, knee, thigh and hamstring areas – and then the right leg. Once you've scanned the legs, move your awareness to the pelvic region, abdomen and chest area, the hands and arms, the back, shoulders, neck, face and head. Investigate each part of the body with a sense of friendliness and warmth – perhaps asking yourself gently, 'What's here, right now?' There's no need to analyse the experience – just allow it to unfold. As best you can, notice the sensations on the inside and outside of your body – can you pay attention to the muscles, organs, bones and skin? Do the sensations you experience change over time, or as you move your attention around?

Whenever the mind wanders away, keep bringing attention back to the part of the body you're focusing on. If you like, you could congratulate yourself for noticing each time the mind has wandered, for that's the moment of coming back into awareness.

When you have scanned each part of the body, gradually expand your attention until it rests on and in the whole of your body. Stay with this whole-body awareness for a while, and then when you are ready to come out of the formal practice, open your eyes. Take a look around at your environment, roll over onto your side and, in your own time, gradually get up.

MINDFULNESS OF BODY: SUGGESTIONS FOR PRACTICE

FALLING AWAKE

Although the body scan is usually done lying down, we are cultivating wakefulness rather than sleepiness. If you have a tendency to fall asleep, try practising with your eyes open. If you are in bed, perhaps move to another location less associated with sleep. The practice can also be done sitting up or even standing. Don't give yourself a hard time for falling asleep – perhaps that's what your body is saying you need. If so, come back to the practice when you are well rested.

NOT 'TRYING' TO RELAX

People often think the body scan is a relaxation exercise, but this idea can create tension, especially if you don't feel relaxed while doing it. Actually, it's an awareness practice – your only job is to notice the sensations in your body as they arise – if you feel relaxed, notice that; if you feel tense, notice that. Sometimes the best way to relax is to let things be as they are.

CULTIVATING ACCEPTANCE

Let go of judging your practice experience as 'good' or 'bad'. If you notice pain or discomfort in some part of the body, experiment with coming up close to it, really experiencing each moment of the discomfort fully. What's the pain like – throbbing, sharp or a dull ache? Does it change over time? Do you notice any desire to get rid of, shut out or escape from it? Are there any mental storylines around the pain, such as 'I hate it,' or 'This will never end'? If so, just notice those, too, as best you can without buying into them. Can you allow them to whirr on in the background while you bring the primary focus of your attention to the body?

If there is discomfort, see if you can treat it with kindness, or even make friends with it. Perhaps say to yourself gently: 'It's OK, this experience is here – let me feel it.' When you treat discomfort like this, what happens? Discomfort during practice doesn't make it a 'bad' meditation – every time you practise with awareness, your practice is a success.

JUST DO IT...

The mind can come up with all sorts of reasons not to practise, or to think that meditation isn't 'working'. But meditation simply brings awareness of what's going on. So if you notice thoughts that say you're not doing it properly, or that you're too tense or distracted, or you can't feel anything, then that's what you've become aware of. Can you let those thoughts rest in your wider field of awareness, and gently return your attention to the body each time you get caught up in them?

ONGOING MINDFULNESS OF BODY

Once you've finished this formal practice, see if you can maintain a sense of body mindfulness as you continue about your day. Check in with your body at regular intervals – you might even want to set your phone or an alarm on your computer, reminding you to notice at regular intervals what your body is saying. Be aware of the tendency to tense up certain areas – the shoulders, jaw or thighs. Allow the tension to drop if it will, but if it won't, don't fight it – just notice that it's there.

Jonty's Experience

Mindfulness of body isn't just about treating illness or managing physical symptoms. Increasing awareness of our bodies, as with our breath, helps anchor us in the present moment. I've found that it's a particularly good practice during exercise. I've always tried to keep physically active, but living in London and not really having a 'runner's physique' means that I tend to rely on going to the gym to keep fit. My usual approach is to spend some time on the treadmill, trying to distract myself from all the unpleasant sensations I'm feeling in my body by listening to music or watching the TV screen above me. Then I go and pull and push, lift and squeeze my muscles on various machines while I daydream about the six-pack I want. It's a pretty mindless process. The simple act of raising my pulse rate will still be benefiting my heart, but this approach to exercise doesn't really engage my body or my mind – if anything, it further disconnects me from my body. I treat it like a machine to be serviced, and in the long term I risk injury and damage rather than health and fitness.

With the help of Julien Diaz, a movement expert, I have recently started to discover that, as a result of not paying attention to my body over time, I have been overusing a lot of the 'wrong' muscles. Years of rowing at school mean that I have been exercising some parts disproportionately. Even during sit-ups I try and work with my shoulders and my legs, not my stomach! As I have become more mindful of my body, I've tried to identify the muscles I use and move effort to my core, gradually loosening my shoulders and hips and using my body in a more efficient way. I am also now able to distinguish the 'good pain' of muscles stretching or working from the 'bad pain' of tension in the wrong places, risking damage.

Julien has helped me to vary what I do, avoid repetitive movements and engage my mind and body in the process. And, of course, the advantage of exercising mindfully is that it also helps me stay in the present moment, not only reducing the risk of injuring myself but also resting my mind from worries about work or what needs doing at home. In this way exercise becomes something I do to take care of myself rather than a punishment for having had an extra chocolate biscuit! So, although I may not have that six-pack I always wanted, I do feel healthier and happier.

. . . .

Ed's Experience

Like Jonty, I've been lucky enough to connect with my body through sport and exercise. I've always enjoyed playing football, tennis and squash – and going running or swimming.

I believe part of the reason I found physical exercise so enjoyable when I was growing up was that it was about the only time I allowed my body and mind to synchronize – as any sportsperson will tell you, it's difficult to play well if your mind is elsewhere. The best players are right 'in the zone' – fully in flow with the direct experience of their minds, bodies and the game.

But it was only when I started meditating that I really
began to pay conscious attention to my body. At first,
it was uncomfortable – I discovered tension in my
shoulders and jaw that had probably always been there,
but which I'd never been really aware of. It was hard to
sit there and accept that my body was not as calm as
I'd thought. But it also made sense of many of the stress
symptoms that I'd manifested over the years – I could
see how bodily tension led to my frequent migraines,
for example. I also realized how my bouts of depression
were far more than a mental phenomenon – my whole
body protested when I was overwhelmed. By becoming
more aware of my body, I gained access to an internal
warning system that tells me when I need to slow
down or take a break. I don't always listen to it – the
compulsion to cram 40 hours' activity into a 24-hour day
is compelling – but I'm now more aware that I have a
choice: before practising meditation, I rarely heard what
my body was saying. My body is no longer a machine to
flog to death.

. . . .

CHAPTER 4

MINDFULNESS OF MIND

Thoughts are not facts, and we are not our thoughts. Knowing this, we can enjoy more flexibility in our minds and lives.

Mental distress is a huge cause of human suffering – the World Health Organization estimates that 450 million people across the globe suffer from a diagnosable psychiatric illness,[1] while studies suggest that around half of us will meet the criteria for a mental health problem at some point in our lives.[2] In predicting that depression will be the world's most common illness by 2030, the WHO suggests the global burden of the condition will be greater than for illnesses such as diabetes, heart disease and cancer.[3] Mental illness is thought to cost the British economy around £100 billion a year.[4]

AN UNHAPPINESS EPIDEMIC

These kinds of statistics are just the tip of the iceberg – how many more of us might not meet the precise criteria for clinical depression, but still wouldn't classify ourselves as happy? Very few people are deeply contented – we feel unfulfilled, insecure or troubled by a sense of inadequacy, or prone to getting tense, argumentative and critical. We focus on our regrets, and worry about missing out on opportunities that may turn into regrets in the future. The relentless pressure of modern life probably contributes to our unhappiness – the speed and distraction of our world doesn't help us feel safe, supported or secure. Many of us now compare our lives, not just to those of neighbours, but to people we've never met – celebrities who seem to epitomize our fantasies of how and who we'd like to be. And so our own achievements are met without enthusiasm; rather than being delighted in, they leave us longing for more.

Despite this pervasive discontent, there's often a fear of addressing the issues around psychological health. Whereas the cast on a broken leg might be proudly displayed for friends to sign, problems like depression still get hidden away. When we admit to difficulties with our minds, there's a tendency to think people see as us as weak, stupid or self-indulgent. Perhaps we've made some progress from the days when the 'mentally ill' were basically discarded, locked up in asylums where no one could see them, but the taboo remains for anyone to measure: just 12 per cent of NHS resources are spent on mental health services.[5] If we pay so little attention to looking after our minds, is it any wonder we're in the midst of a misery epidemic?

Why are we so reluctant to take care of our minds? Ironically, it could be because we're so caught up with them. While we objectify our bodies, tending to see them as something we own rather than something we are, with our minds it's somewhat different. We interpret the world with our thoughts, so aren't our thoughts who we really are? Aren't my thoughts 'me'? And if my thoughts are 'me', then isn't it distressing and embarrassing when they won't do what I want, and I don't seem to be in charge of my mind?

Our culture prizes thinking – ideas, logic and analysis are valued as ways to manage life, make progress and achieve mastery. We like to see ourselves as rational creatures, able to solve difficulties through the power of analysis. Mental capacity seems to be a defining feature of our sophistication as a species. As Descartes put it, 'I think, therefore I am.'

Thought is essential – it's the basis for many of the great advances humanity has made over the centuries. But just as our relationship with the body is out of balance, could our relationship with thinking also be out of whack, with similarly stressful consequences? In this case, might it be that we're so identified with our minds and their busyness that we're unable to take a realistic perspective on them, too caught up to discover that – maybe – we are not our thoughts in the way we imagine?

When we get distracted from the present moment, where does the mind go? When we find ourselves obsessing about the past, dreaming about the future or wishing things were different in the here and now, what actually happens? If you've been working with the mindfulness of breathing and body practices we've introduced so far, you may have found that your attention wanders most commonly into thought. When we aren't present to what's happening in our lives, it's usually because we get trapped in our heads, holed up in mental concepts about what's going on rather than actually experiencing it directly. We don't choose to do this – it just happens.

Remember the banana example from Chapter 1? It's difficult for us to experience the actual banana in front of us because we're so often tied up in thoughts that take us away from direct perception. So when we pick up the banana, we start having all sorts of thoughts and judgements about it: 'It's not as ripe as the one I had yesterday,' or 'I really hate fruit – what I actually want is a delicious chocolate muffin!' Or maybe we get carried away by thoughts that have nothing to do with the banana at all – we're so stuck on rehashing an argument we had earlier or worrying about the presentation we've got to make that we hardly notice what's in front of us at all. When we get caught in thought, it takes us away from the reality of our experience, right here, right now.

We're encouraged to identify with thought as proof of our independence and self-control, but given that the mind constantly strays into abstract flights of fancy, perhaps this isn't so wise. Actually, isn't it more often that we are led by our thoughts, driven unconsciously to where they want us to go? Don't our thoughts think us, more than we think them?

If we don't see that we're not always masters of our thoughts, they can lead us further into the territory of depression – telling us we're bad, incompetent, lazy and unlikable – and we end up believing that it's all our fault. We identify with what our minds are telling us, because we think the thoughts are ours. Cue further blame, self-hatred, anger, resistance – and stress.

OUR SKEWED PERCEPTIONS

It doesn't help that our thoughts are habitually geared towards the negative. This is partly an evolutionary legacy – because early humans had to be ready to ward off attacks from predators, we're more sensitized to perceived threats than to pleasant stimuli. If our ancestors failed to notice something nice (a beautiful sunset, say) that might have been a shame, but not the immediate catastrophe of failing to see a lion hiding in the undergrowth. When something unpleasant happens – or looks like it might happen – we are primed to pay attention to it, and to focus on it. We're programmed to fear the worst, and because our perceptions are skewed, we tend to catastrophize, worry, criticize and judge, based not just on the facts, but with a strong negative bias. A lot of us see things as worse than they are, especially when we're under stress.

Our worrying thoughts then act in tandem with body reactions – we tense up and brace until the problem passes or we can find a way out of it. But just as tensing up the body in reaction to chronic stress isn't very helpful, so rumination is also a poor way of dealing with most of our modern-day worries – we can't always think our way out of a difficult situation. When thought doesn't produce a solution, rumination just leads us to become more and more preoccupied. We churn the problem over and over in our minds, fretting endlessly, trying to work out what to do. This crowds out perspectives that might lead to a lightening of our mood or some life-enhancing action.

Instead of helping us resolve the problem we're facing, rumination tends to make us more and more distracted, tired and introspective – and more and more focused on our (unhappy) selves. We get trapped in our heads, and our minds and bodies stay locked in a state of tension, unconsciously conspiring to keep us driven and anxious.

We are most of us prone to these patterns, but those of us who get most hooked on negative thinking patterns – due to genetic inheritance, past influences and current life circumstances – are also most vulnerable to conditions like depression. The cycle can get worse over time, too – each episode of distress seems to get stored in us as a memory, and we're likely to become even more sensitive to similar situations in the future.[6] Around half the people who get depressed will have another episode at some point, while a person who's been depressed three or more times is 90 per cent likely to relapse.[7] Repeated episodes can be triggered by the fearful messages stored from previous experiences – typical depressive thoughts such as: 'Here we go again!', 'I never handle these things well!' or 'Other people cope better than me – I'm such a loser!' contribute to making another episode more likely, as well as having a negative impact on health generally. Research suggests that later episodes of depression can actually be triggered by worry and rumination alone, even when there hasn't been a crisis to set them off. It's the Buddha's second arrow again – we experience not just the pain of our current situation, but the stress laid onto it by our negative interpretations.

WORKING SKILFULLY WITH THOUGHTS

Treatments for depression – such as cognitive therapy – focus on helping people challenge their negative thoughts and perceptions. They encourage us to understand how, under stress, the mind interprets everything through a distorted mirror, making things look worse than they actually are. These approaches aim to help us to ignore, question or change our thoughts when they aren't based in reality.

But it's not easy to alter mental patterns we've been practising all our lives. If we're used to being tied up in negative thinking, that habit is likely to be deeply ingrained in us, and our thoughts may not respond when we tell them to do something different. We are trying to use our mind to change our mind – and that's not easy. Challenging negative thoughts can sometimes be a useful strategy, but if we are unable to change or push away thoughts, there's a danger that we might become even more depressed, perhaps aggressively blaming our mind for not being more accurate, or ourselves for not being stronger or more positive. When we fight with our minds like this, it can lead to the same problem chronic pain patients have with their bodies: battling unpleasant experiences, or trying to get rid of them, can actually make things worse.

So perhaps we need a slightly different approach. In order not to get hooked on our inaccurate thoughts, perhaps we don't need to challenge or change them, so much as simply see them for what they are – just thoughts. Rather than trying to alter the content of the mind, perhaps we could find another perspective, seeing these thoughts from a different angle.

In the mindfulness-based stress-reduction programme, Jon Kabat-Zinn taught his chronic pain patients a new way of working not just with their bodily pain, but with the mental distress that so often comes with it. When pain was accompanied by a stressful narrative, the instruction was simply to notice this storyline and come back to awareness of the breath or body. Through dis-identifying with habitual thoughts about pain, MBSR participants learn that thoughts can be observed without being believed. Through the practice of meditation, they train in being able to make this distinction.

Western psychology calls this ability *meta-cognition*. With meta-cognition, we relate *to* rather than *from* our thoughts. We aren't able to do much about what our thoughts tell us – they tend to keep whirring away, regardless of any attempts we make to stop them. But we can become skilled at choosing when to listen, and when to treat thoughts as harmless background noise. When we're able to recognize that our perceptions are inaccurate, we are starting to use the part of the mind that sees through habitual assumptions and helps us observe situations clearly. With this awareness, we can release the powerful grip that thoughts have on us. We can start to see that thoughts are not facts, and that we don't have to believe everything we think…

VISITORS TO THE STRESS REDUCTION CLINIC

If practising meditation helps chronic pain patients cultivate meta-cognition, could it also help people who experience depression? In the mid-1990s, the stress reduction clinic at the University of Massachusetts hosted a series of visits from Mark Williams and John Teasdale from Cambridge University, and Zindel Segal from Toronto's Clarke Institute of Psychiatry. Williams, Teasdale and Segal are cognitive psychologists, and they were working to develop new treatments for depression. They had been asked to devise a group version of cognitive therapy, aimed at helping people who'd been depressed several times. They were especially focused on helping people free themselves from the relapsing cycle of depression, in which negative thinking leads from one bout to the next.

The three had heard about Jon Kabat-Zinn through a colleague, and realized that his mindfulness instructions might be just what their depressed patients needed. Their visits to Massachusetts gave them cause for optimism – observing the mindfulness-based stress-reduction programme, they saw ordinary people with chronic health problems learning to deal with their situation in a new and often life-changing way.

As respected psychologists, they were a bit concerned about how their colleagues might react to the idea of using mindfulness, especially to treat an intractable condition like depression. Mark Williams remembers being accosted at a conference and asked incredulously: 'Is it really true what I hear, that John Teasdale is *meditating* with his patients?'

Nevertheless, they decided to trust the research from the stress reduction clinic, as well as their own experience of the programme in action. For the next several years, they dedicated themselves to adapting the MBSR programme specifically for people at risk of depression.

The new course was called Mindfulness-Based Cognitive Therapy (MBCT). It retained all the main elements of MBSR, and also introduced some tools and techniques from cognitive therapy. These included role-play exercises to show how negative thinking can make moods worse, and asking participants to write relapse-prevention plans to put in place when they spot the warning signs of depression approaching.

Although it was meant for people with a 'mental' health problem, MBCT retained a strong emphasis on attention to the body. The clear distinction we tend to make between 'mental' and 'physical' health problems is a false one – despite the name we give it, mental health doesn't just happen in the head. People who are depressed often suffer heart palpitations, headaches, muscle tension, churning stomachs, tiredness and poor appetite. They also frequently lose touch with their bodies, especially when they get tied up in thoughts. The reaction to bodily symptoms can be more worry and rumination, and more dissociation, which in turn provokes yet more physical distress. By encouraging participants to anchor themselves in the present moment, to be more in their bodies, there might be some release from this cycle.

The mindfulness practices taught in the MBCT programme all facilitate a shift in perspective. Through mindfulness of breathing, participants are invited to place attention on something other than thoughts, to be less tied up in rumination and to come down into their bodily experience. Mindfulness of body takes this process further, enabling them to become more attuned to the physical signs that can herald the onset of depression, rather than being drawn into a ruminative cycle of despair. And through being mindful of thoughts themselves – watching them in meditation – participants learn to observe the thinking process from a more helpful vantage point, seeing and accepting thoughts with kindly awareness, but not making the mistake of always believing they are true.

KATHY'S EXPERIENCE

Kathy, 47, was referred to an MBCT course three years ago. She says mindfulness has been the missing piece in her mental health jigsaw…

Kathy has a long history of depression. About 12 years ago she was prescribed medication, and the drugs seemed to bring her some stability. As she gradually improved, she talked with her GP about finding new ways to cope. Her doctor referred her to a cognitive behavioural therapist, and she also went to see a nutritionist.

One day she was chatting with a friend who mentioned mindfulness training – the friend raved about how much she had benefited from it. Kathy mentioned mindfulness to her therapist, who was able to refer her onto a course.

At the first session, the teacher led the group in a 'body scan'. Kathy immediately thought: 'Yes, I can do this!' 'That doesn't mean it was easy,' she adds. 'It was quite a challenge to make time to do the practice every day. But it felt like something I could manage.' Slowly but surely, as the weeks went by, Kathy began to feel something changing for her. 'I started to be able to recognize more of my own issues – particularly my tendency to want to do everything right. It was quite painful to see it come up during the meditation sessions, but I felt something shifting in me.'

It wasn't long before Kathy really began to feel the benefits of her training. 'Towards the end of the course, or it might have been just afterwards, I took a Saturday morning continuing education class. For the first time in one of those lessons, I really felt I could be there mentally. I wasn't feeling guilty for not doing something else, like staying at home with my family. Mindfulness has given me the ability to feel more connected – to more fully be wherever I am. One of my kids asked me why I was doing the course and I said I was learning how to pay attention. They thought it was really stupid, but that sums it up for me – you're learning how to recognize what's going on, internally and externally.'

MBCT has had a big impact on how Kathy handles her moods. 'I've got my medication down as low as it's ever been and I haven't had a major depression since the course. Unpleasant feelings and stress still come, but I'm not engaging with them like I used to. If I get delayed when I really need to be somewhere else, I don't waste all my energy worrying about it – I can say: "OK, I'm here now, so let's make the most of it." And I'm more OK when I've had a really stressful week.'

A good example of how practising mindfulness helps Kathy came when she and her family went to London for some Christmas shopping. 'We were in a big toy department and it was really busy,' she remembers. 'I don't usually do crowds well – I don't like the pressure and stress. I started getting anxious about losing one of the kids – I basically had a kind of panic attack. But I know that when things get hard, I need to pay attention to what my body is doing. So, I started saying to myself: "OK, my heart rate and blood pressure are going up, I'm feeling very tense and my shoulders are tightening." Just that process helped me back up a little bit – I didn't go into a full panic attack, even though I'd been verging on it. I think if I hadn't had the mindfulness training to help me think a bit differently, I probably wouldn't have been able to ward it off. Being able to recognize experiences in my body is enough to stop me getting sucked into my old patterns, blaming and judging myself.'

Like most of us, Kathy leads a busy life and has lots of responsibilities. Having a family to look after doesn't leave her with a lot of spare time, but she knows that she needs to meditate to keep her mind in good shape. 'A little bit of practice every day makes a huge amount of difference,' she says.

Kathy had tried lots of ways of coping with depression – many of them helpful. But she says MBCT has made the most difference. 'I've done a lot of talk therapy, but mindfulness has made the bigger shift, probably because of the way it helps you pay attention and take that step back. For me, at least, depression comes from getting overwhelmed with pain or frustration or irritability, and I'm not participating in those feelings the way I used to. I think mindfulness is the piece that's missing in other kinds of psychotherapy.'

SCIENTIFIC TESTING

To convince a potentially sceptical medical establishment, the developers of MBCT knew they had to test their treatment scientifically. Does Mindfulness-Based Cognitive Therapy actually help people at risk of depression to stay well? To find out, they carried out a trial, conducted jointly at their universities in Toronto, Cambridge and Bangor (Mark Williams had by this time moved from Cambridge to North Wales).[8] They randomly allocated 145 patients at high risk of depression to one of two groups: one set was put through a course of Mindfulness-Based Cognitive Therapy, while the others carried on receiving their usual treatment. The progress of both groups was then measured over the following year.

The results were clear: of the patients who had suffered more than two episodes of depression (three-quarters of them), just over a third in the MBCT group relapsed over the next year. But for those who had not received mindfulness training, the relapse rate was twice as high – two-thirds became depressed again. MBCT had made a significant difference – doubling people's chances of staying well. In 2004, a second trial produced more positive results: of those most prone to depression, 36 per cent of the MBCT participants relapsed, compared to 78 per cent for the control group.[9]

As a result of these two studies, Mindfulness-Based Cognitive Therapy received an important endorsement. In the UK, a body called the National Institute for Health and Clinical Excellence (NICE) decides which treatments should be offered on the National Health Service – its decisions are based on the best available scientific evidence. In 2004, NICE recommended MBCT for people who have suffered more than two episodes of depression. This made mindfulness part of official UK health policy, a Government-approved treatment for depression alongside more established medical approaches such as antidepressant drugs and psychological therapies. Meditation was starting to emerge from the fringes of medicine – mindfulness was going mainstream.

The scientific evidence that mindfulness aids wellbeing has kept on coming. In 2007, a team led by Professor Willem Kuyken at Exeter University carried out another trial, this time comparing MBCT with the most commonly used treatment – antidepressant drugs.[10] Kuyken and his colleagues followed 123 people who had a history of recurrent depression and were taking antidepressants as a 'maintenance' treatment. This means that they were being prescribed the drugs long-term, in the hope of maintaining a chemical balance to protect them from relapse. The patients were either given MBCT (in which case they were also invited to come off the pills) or asked to continue as usual with their drug treatment.

In the year following the course, 60 per cent of the non-MBCT group relapsed, compared to 47 per cent of those who were taught mindfulness (three-quarters of whom also stopped taking antidepressants). The study found that mindfulness was better at preventing relapse and more likely to improve the participants' quality of life. MBCT was also more cost-effective than antidepressants, with a likelihood of greater savings over a longer period of time. This is because mindfulness training doesn't usually have to be 're-prescribed' like pills – patients can continue to practise at home, after the course is over, using the skills they have learned.

The comparison with antidepressant treatment was also explored in a trial whose results were published at the end of 2010 – it found that people given mindfulness therapy did as well as those who took drugs (both groups relapsed at a rate of around 30 per cent over 18 months). This was compared to another group who were given just placebo pills – more than 70 per cent of these patients relapsed over the same time period.[11]

There have been several small trials offering MBCT as a treatment for people when they are actually depressed, rather than when they are in between episodes. The results from these are encouraging, too – in one, MBCT reduced people's symptoms of depression from severe to mild (compared to no change in a group who didn't receive the training), while another found that a third of patients were no longer depressed at the end of the course.[12]

Jon Kabat-Zinn's research indicated that MBSR could also reduce anxiety,[13] and there have now been enough studies of mindfulness and mood to make it the subject of some meta-analyses, in which the results of a number of trial results are combined to draw more confident conclusions. One review examined 39 sets of data and concluded that mindfulness is effective for managing both depression and anxiety.[14] Interestingly, the authors of the paper admitted they were sceptical when they began their review, expecting to find that the course had either little or no effect. The evidence they encountered changed their minds – they ended up praising mindfulness as a 'promising intervention'. There have also been encouraging trials of mindfulness-based approaches for people with other psychological issues, including obsessive-compulsive disorder,[15] attention-deficit hyperactivity disorder,[16] and generalized anxiety disorder.[17]

The benefits of mindfulness aren't limited to those working with a clinical diagnosis. Remember the study Jon Kabat-Zinn carried out with office workers in Madison, Wisconsin? Over the duration of the course, those who learned meditation climbed 20 places out of 100 in a ranking of happiness.[18] Other trials with generally healthy populations have also shown benefits such as reduced stress levels and improved sleep quality.[19] The evidence shows that, through meditation practice, we can all learn to work with our minds more skilfully.

HOW DOES MINDFULNESS HELP?

So what does the science tell us about *how* mindfulness helps? First, with meditation training it seems people can relate to thoughts with greater awareness. A study led by

John Teasdale found that when MBCT reduced relapse among people prone to depression, it also increased their meta-cognitive abilities, suggesting that it may indeed be a changing relationship with thought that brings some of the benefit.[20] Several subsequent studies have also suggested that people are less tied up in their thoughts – they ruminate less – after they've been on a mindfulness course.[21]

More evidence that living in a mindful way is beneficial comes from an innovative Harvard study. Researchers tracked the activities of over 2,000 participants by asking them to record what was going on for them several times a day, as prompted by an alarm on their iPhones. It found that their minds wandered from what they were doing almost half of the time, but that participants were happier when engaged with what was happening in the present moment. In fact, how often people's minds wandered was a better predictor of happiness than the kind of activities they were actually undertaking.[22]

Science is also confirming that mindfulness helps people relate more compassionately to their experience. Whereas ruminative thinking is often critical, harsh and unkind, the awareness cultivated in mindfulness is gentle, warm and friendly. So at the same time as learning not to identify with our critical inner voice, mindfulness seems to nurture a more caring way of being with ourselves. Another of Willem Kuyken's studies suggests this might be partly why MBCT is effective – the programme protects people from relapsing into depression by inviting them to practise self-compassion.[23]

BEING YOUR OWN GOOD PARENT

A helpful way to visualize this is as a kind of 'self-parenting'. By learning how to develop a non-critical 'observing' part of our mind and using it to watch, hold and be kind to our thoughts, no matter how unpleasant they seem, we are looking after ourselves just like a good mother or father looks after a child – with attention, patience and love. We are offering kindness to our thoughts even when they misinform or frustrate us – leading us to panic or give up, perhaps. We aren't pushing them away or criticizing them, nor are we buying into the inaccurate stories they tell us. We are offering simply to hold them in awareness.

Psychologists have long said that a child needs this kind of relationship with caregivers to grow into a psychologically healthy adult. A child who receives mindful attention develops what is known as 'secure attachment' – they learn to trust the world around them and, as they grow up, to trust themselves. 'Securely attached' people feel confident about trying new experiences, making friends and dealing with life's setbacks. To be fundamentally happy, they are not dependent on the opinions of others or on everything always going well in their lives.

On the other hand, if a child doesn't get this kind of care, they may never learn to feel safe and comforted, or how to regulate their thoughts, feelings and behaviour. They may be unable to look after themselves, and feel frightened, lonely and under-confident a lot of the time. They may lack good boundaries, and live a chaotic life. They might have a 'fragile ego', always needing other people to like them, worried that something bad is going to happen or that they won't be able to cope on their own. Insecurely attached people never learn to internalize a 'good parent' because they did not experience this quality of care as a child.

Modern researchers have noted the similarities between the qualities possessed by people who are 'securely attached' and those who are more mindful. Naturally mindful people (those who possess a high degree of what psychologists call 'trait' or 'dispositional' mindfulness) have been shown in tests to be less prone to psychological distress, including depression and anxiety, as well as being less neurotic and more extroverted. They also enjoy a greater sense of wellbeing: reporting more joy, contentment and satisfaction with life.[24]

Naturally mindful people recover from sad moods more quickly, ruminate less and are less likely to shy away from difficult experiences – they are also not as perfectionist. They have fewer negative thoughts and tend not to get so hung up on them. And they have greater self-esteem which is less dependent on things going well in their lives – they are not so shattered by difficult experiences, and know how to look after themselves when under pressure.[25]

Mindfulness practice can help us grow our own internal 'good parent', even when we become adults. By offering kindly attention to ourselves in the present moment, we are learning how to relate to our experience with gentleness, even when things are difficult. This image of mindfulness as compassionate self-parenting also appears in some traditional meditation teachings, which speak of 'placing the mind of fearfulness in the cradle of loving-kindness'.[26]

DIXON'S EXPERIENCE

When Dixon signed up for a Mindfulness-Based Cognitive Therapy course, he hoped to learn techniques to deal with depression. He did – but mindfulness has helped him cope with a lot more than just his low moods…

Dixon, now in his mid-50s, has suffered from depression since he was a teenager, but he says his difficulties really came to the fore after he had Q fever – a bacterial infection with symptoms similar to severe flu, and which also affects the liver. 'From then on', he says, 'my health was never the same.' Also diagnosed with chronic fatigue, Dixon soldiered on working as a teacher, but says he was often depressed and tired.

His doctor suggested a course of Mindfulness-Based Cognitive Therapy. At first, Dixon was unsure. 'If I'd been asked about meditation before that, I'd have remembered my youth and The Beatles and thought: "Yes, well, that's OK for a bunch of long-haired hippies, but it's not for me!"' Nevertheless, he decided he had nothing to lose. 'I thought: "Well, let's give it a go – the worst that can happen is you go along a couple of times and if everyone's burning incense and wearing kaftans, you can walk away." But it wasn't like that.'

Dixon says that MBCT gave him both an understanding of depression and the tools to deal with it. 'I learned how depression affects people like me, and how to recognize the problems before they become serious. Depression consists of the mind wandering into areas that it shouldn't go, either reviewing painful or unpleasant things from the past or considering fears for the future. With practice you become aware of what your mind is doing – you notice: "Oh yes, I'm thinking about something that I don't need to be thinking about." That's a terrific weapon against depression.

'Once you have a regular meditation practice, you can say: "I'm in charge of my life." I know that sounds strange, but I don't think I was before. I wasn't in charge of my mind – it went and did its own thing, and I wasn't aware that I was recycling a lot of stuff and making myself very anxious and worried. Depression makes people focus on themselves and their own problems to the point that they stop functioning. Mindfulness stops you from doing that. You don't allow your mind to tie you up.'

Two years ago, Dixon's mindfulness training became even more relevant. He was admitted to hospital with severe back pain, and doctors told him he had bone cancer – there were three shattered vertebrae where his spine had eroded. He now uses the 'mental tools' he learned in MBCT to deal with the challenges of living with cancer.

'When I did the course', he explains, 'I had no inkling that I had other medical issues, but mindfulness has helped a lot in coping with pain. Through meditation you examine the nature of pain and discomfort and get up close to it – you find out about it. And surprisingly, the closer you get the more you are able to deal with it. If I have pains in my lower back or my pelvis I can sit there and pay attention to it – surprisingly often, you realize the pain isn't as dreadful as you thought. We think that hurting is hurting, but it's how you perceive it. A lot of pain is down to what's in your mind. That's quite strange – five years ago if somebody had said that to me I'd have been like: "Cobblers! If it hurts, it hurts!"'

Dixon has recently had major surgery to repair his spine, along with chemotherapy and a stem cell transplant – when he was in the hospital, he would sit on his bed and use the mindfulness practices he learned on the course, and he prioritizes them when he's at home, usually managing to practise formally for about half an hour, four times a week. 'I'm not only dealing with depression now,' he explains. 'I'm also dealing with all the fears that go with a serious, long-term illness. Meditation helps me calm my mind and focus and make sure that I don't panic or overreact. It's helped me come to terms with the problem that I've got and how to deal with it.

'By focusing on the here and now, you're dealing not with the fear about "What's going to happen to my family?" and all the other things that weigh you down, but "How are things right at this moment?" That's a wonderful thing to be able to do – a lifeline. My son is 11 years old and he needs a dad who can take him to his football training and tell jokes – MBCT has given me the courage and fortitude to do that. It sets my mind up to crack on with life rather than sinking into a swamp of despondency.'

MEDITATION ON THE BRAIN

The science of mindfulness is also beginning to tell us what's happening in our heads when we meditate. Just as material signs of practice are evident in the body, so there is evidence of a corresponding transformation in the functioning – and even structure – of the brain.

Until recently, the idea that we can affect the make-up of the brain through behaviour wasn't much entertained in scientific circles. Of course it was widely accepted that the condition of our brain affects how we experience the world – if it suffered damage from a car accident or a stroke, for example, it would likely have an impact on your ability to think or to perform actions which would previously have been easy for you. However, the possibility that this could work the other way round – that we might be able to influence the structure of the brain by how we use our minds – that seemed pretty unlikely.

The old orthodoxy was that brain structure was firmly fixed by the time we became adults – once childhood was over, you were basically stuck with what you already had. One consequence of this in terms of our wellbeing was an understanding that adults have a fairly stable 'happiness set-point'.[27] While our day-to-day experience of mood goes up and down, fluctuating according to what we're doing and what happens to us, our basic predisposition towards cheeriness or gloom was thought to be basically unalterable. It was noticed that even if something really wonderful or really awful happened to a person, the effect on their happiness was usually short-lived. So when someone won the lottery, for instance, their mood would go up for a while, but within a year or two they were usually about as happy or unhappy as they were prior to the windfall.[28] Similarly, when someone had an accident that left them in a wheelchair, they felt more miserable than usual for a while, but then would return to their usual mood range. But thanks to technology enabling researchers to look closely at what the brain is doing, scientists now think the happiness set-point isn't quite as 'set' as it seemed.

NEUROPLASTICITY

Techniques such as electro-encephalography (EEG) allow us to study electrical activity in the brain, while Functional Magnetic Resonance Imaging (fMRI) lets us look in great detail at which parts of the brain are most active when we're carrying out certain tasks. Information and images from these studies have allowed neuroscientists to discover and map how regions of the brain 'light up' when we learn a new language, solve a maths problem or think about someone we know.

These methods have taught us a lot about how the brain works, and we now know that structural changes can and do occur throughout our lifetime – fresh connections are made between neurons, and around 5,000 new neurons are created every day. Thanks to the new scanning techniques, neuroscientists have shown that changes occur as a result of whatever we do in our lives. The brain is constantly rewiring and reshaping itself in response to experience – a phenomenon known as *neuroplasticity*.

A famous example of this is a study that scanned the brains of London taxi drivers, and discovered that, on average, cabbies have a larger hippocampus than the rest of us.[29] The hippocampus is a part of the brain associated with spatial processing and memory, skills that taxi drivers might be expected to practise regularly, given that they have to navigate complex street configurations as they ferry people around a large, sprawling city. Could it be that taxi drivers have larger hippocampi because they have to carry out intensive memorization exercises when they train to do their job, and then continue to use that part of the brain regularly whenever they're at work?

It seems highly likely that it's the taxi driver's job that makes this difference to their brain – researchers found that the hippocampi of cabbies who'd been doing the job longer are larger than those of newly qualified drivers. Similar evidence of neuroplasticity has been found in other studies, too – people who speak several languages have larger brains in areas that relate to word processing,[30] while the brains of musicians who play stringed instruments are different in the regions that control fine motor movement.[31]

Neuroplasticity seems to work a bit like body conditioning. Nobody gets very surprised that lifting heavy weights can make the muscles in your arms grow stronger, so is it really strange that engaging in mental exercise strengthens the brain in the same way? Perhaps not, but until the phenomenon of neuroplasticity became detectable through technology, there was no obvious evidence that this might be the case. The fact that we can now say this happens has big ramifications – it suggests that qualities of mind like attention, empathy or joy can be developed like muscles in our bodies. We can train ourselves to be wiser and more content.

Of course, just as all the weight training in the world won't turn an 8-stone guy into a heavyweight boxing champion, so we all have predispositions towards particular qualities of character, including how happy we are. However, the existence of neuroplasticity indicates that these predispositions may not be as determined as once thought. By training ourselves to relate with experience differently – even when we are adults – we can begin to free ourselves from patterns that appear to be fixed, either genetically or in early life. As we practise in this way, new neuronal tracks are created in our brains. We have some power to shape our destiny.

THE NEUROSCIENCE OF MEDITATION

The question, then, is can mindfulness change the brain in ways that help us live more contented lives? At the Laboratory for Affective Neuroscience at the University of Wisconsin, Professor Richard Davidson has been investigating the neuroscience of meditation for the best part of two decades.[32] His research suggests not only that significant brain changes occur as a result of practice, but also that these changes are associated with greater wellbeing.

First of all, Davidson found a way to tell how happy a person generally is by analysing the electrical activity in their brain, using EEG readings. He took hundreds of readings from different people, and found that when they are upset, anxious or depressed they tend to exhibit more activity in certain areas – most notably the right prefrontal cortex, which is located just behind the forehead.[33] He also found that when people are more upbeat, there is more activity in the left prefrontal cortex, and less going on in the right prefrontal cortex.

Davidson used his readings to predict people's basic mood tendencies – the more activity they generally show on the right, the likelier they are to have a gloomy outlook and shy away from things, while the more activity they show on the left, the more content a person tends to be, and the more inclined they are to 'approach' and be interested in new experiences. Those who show most extreme activity on the right are more likely to have had clinical depression or an anxiety disorder at some point in their lives.

All this might seem to support the idea of a fixed happiness set-point. But what happens if someone engages in a regime of mindfulness meditation? Training in mindfulness involves learning how to 'approach' what's going on in our minds and bodies with curiosity and interest rather than avoiding it, so could it shift that set-point? To find out, Richard Davidson worked alongside Jon Kabat-Zinn on the trial of mindfulness with office workers in Madison, Wisconsin,[34] taking EEG readings from their brains both before and after they'd taken the MBSR course.

Before the course, Davidson's readings suggested that, on average, the workers were at the more unhappy end of the scale – there was more activity than average in their right prefrontal cortexes. Following the mindfulness training, however, not only did they report feeling more positive, more energetic, more engaged in their work and less stressed, but the readings from their brains had changed as well: there was more activity in their left prefrontal cortexes than before, and less activity in the right. The subjects were tested again after another four months – remarkably, the changes had been sustained. This was significant – it suggested that learning mindfulness skills, even over just a couple of months, could have a sustained effect on brain functioning.

Dr Sara Lazar is another neuroscientist who has studied the effect of meditation on the brain, and her studies suggest that mindfulness practice can have a structural impact. She used MRI scans to look at the brains of those who had practised mindfulness for many years, and compared them to people with no meditation experience.[35] The results show that areas of the brain cortex associated with sensory processing and wellbeing were thicker in the meditators, with the difference in cortical thickness greatest in those subjects who had been practising the longest. This suggests that training in mindfulness may have bulked up the meditators' brains, just as a programme of physical training can bulk up the body.

In a further study, Lazar and colleagues showed that the structure of the brain can change even during the eight weeks of a mindfulness course (with an average daily practice time of around half an hour). By taking before-and-after scans, they found that grey matter in parts of the participants' brains had increased in density by 1–3 per cent, affecting areas known to be implicated in learning and memory, as well as self-awareness, compassion and introspection. No similar changes were found in a control group of people who didn't take the course.[36]

MENTAL FLOSS

The scientific evidence suggests that mindfulness is basic mental hygiene – it can help do for your mind what brushing your teeth does for your dental health. Most of us don't think twice about brushing our teeth every day – we learn from an early age that if we don't want tooth decay, regular brushing is essential. But is neglecting your teeth really worse than neglecting your mind? Isn't it strange that we pay more daily attention to caring for the enamel on our teeth than we do our minds? All the evidence suggests that meditation practice can help liberate us from the automatic thoughts and perspectives that so often dominate us, shifting our experience towards greater wellbeing and contentment. No matter how mentally healthy or content we consider ourselves to be, is there anyone who wouldn't benefit from that?

PRACTICE: *Mindfulness of Mind*

In this practice, we turn our attention to the thinking process itself – we watch the contents of our mind with awareness, training to see them from a mindful perspective.

STEP ONE
First, settle into mindfulness of breathing, as described in Chapter 2. Allow yourself some time for each of the steps.

STEP TWO

Now, shift your attention to thoughts, noticing them in the same way as you've practised being aware of the breath or body sensations. What thoughts are present right now? Are they moving through your mind quickly, or do they seem to stick around for a while? Are there a few types of thought that predominate or return frequently (and if so, are they the same every time or a little different?), or are there lots of thoughts that rattle through and seem unconnected? Do your thoughts seem light or heavy? Are there any spaces between them? How is it to be paying attention to thoughts in this way?

STEP THREE

Whenever you notice that your mind has wandered away from watching thoughts – perhaps you suddenly realize that you've become caught up in an idea, or the mind has drifted onto something else (a sound or body sensation, perhaps) – just acknowledge that your mind has wandered and gently bring your attention back to observing thoughts.

STEP FOUR

Continue working with thoughts in this way – as events that come and go in the mind – for the period you have chosen. Working mindfully with thoughts in this way can be challenging, so it's good to practise this for a short period within a longer session. It's fine to return to mindfulness of breathing or body at any time – bringing attention down into the body can help us re-centre when we get distracted by a thought.

ANALOGIES FOR WORKING WITH THOUGHTS

Because we are so used to identifying with our thoughts, sometimes it's difficult to separate them from the wider awareness that can observe thought. There are several analogies that can help with this – you might want to use them as visualizations when you practise.

THE SKY-LIKE NATURE OF AWARENESS

Awareness is sometimes described as being 'sky-like' – with thoughts passing through it like clouds. Some clouds may seem dark and ominous, others light and fluffy. The sky can be totally covered with clouds, or there might be just one or two wispy streaks across the horizon. The clouds are constantly changing shape and appearance as they float by. But no matter what kind of weather there is, beyond these clouds our sky of awareness is always clear.

TRAINSPOTTING

Working with thoughts is also a bit like watching trains at a railway station. We can stand on the platform and see how the trains arrive, stay awhile and then switch tracks and move off into the distance. As we meditate, we practise watching trains of thought pass through, without jumping into the carriage. Whenever we find we have hopped onto a train and it's carrying us away, we can step off again and walk back to the platform.

AT THE THEATRE

Watching a play or a film, we sit in our seat and enjoy the display in front of us. We're not detached from what's going on, but we don't have to believe what we're seeing is real.

We don't get up on the stage or screen and try to join in the dialogue. Similarly, when we're practising mindfulness of mind, we're staying in our spectator's seat, seeing the show that thoughts are putting on for us.

ON THE BANK OF THE RIVER

Do you ever sit by the bank of a river and watch all the flotsam and jetsam pass by? You might see objects you're interested in (fish, leaves, the branch of a tree) and objects you don't like the look of (dirty plastic bottles or sewage). Noticing your reaction to each, observe them all passing by, sometimes as a trickle, sometimes a torrent. In mindfulness practice we can stand on the riverbank of our mind, watching pleasant, unpleasant and neutral thoughts float through.

MINDFULNESS OF MIND: SUGGESTIONS FOR WORKING WITH THOUGHTS

DON'T TRY TO STOP THINKING

There's a common myth that meditation means having a blank mind, or trying to stop your thoughts. But thoughts are not the enemy – trying to stop them will just lead to more struggle. In mindfulness of breathing or body, working with thoughts is a bit like having the radio on in the background – you can hear it, but your main focus is elsewhere. In mindfulness of mind practice, you're paying attention to it, but you're not always buying into what's being said.

FEELING OVERWHELMED BY THOUGHTS

You may feel there are lots of thoughts in your mind when you start to practise. It can be a bit like stepping off a merry-go-round – at first, you feel dizzy, but that's because you've suddenly stopped spinning around in circles. Similarly, when we sit down to meditate we're dropping our speed, and in the stillness it can feel like our minds are more chaotic than usual. But it's not that we're having more thoughts, it's that we're becoming more aware of them. Just as the dizziness of coming off a merry-go-round wears off in time, so the more we practise meditation, the more our minds can begin to settle.

NOT JUDGING THOUGHTS

In meditation, thoughts aren't viewed as 'good' or 'bad'. See if you can cultivate an attitude of equanimity to whatever goes through your mind when you practise – watching your thoughts with curiosity, friendliness and kindness, even when you don't like them.

ACCEPTING THAT THE MIND GETS CAUGHT UP IN THOUGHTS

It's tempting to criticize ourselves when the mind wanders away from an object of meditation. But this happens to everyone – it's part of the practice. Mind-wandering is an opportunity to be gentle with yourself – if your mind didn't wander, you wouldn't be able to practise bringing it back. Remember to congratulate yourself sometimes, when you notice your mind has got caught up. This moment of noticing is the moment of returning to mindfulness.

Jonty's Experience

While I wouldn't consider myself to have a 'mental health problem', ask anyone who knows me and they'll tell you I'm a bit of a worrier. I'm also a perfectionist (the two seem to go hand in hand). These traits have been with me a very long time, and I've spent some time with a therapist exploring why I am this way. However, what seems more important is how I relate to these characteristics and what impact they have on my life right now. For me they've always felt destructive – constantly trying to do so much and having to keep on top of so many different things feels stressful – like being constantly afraid of dropping something. However, for my patients these could be seen as good qualities in their doctor – the last thing any of us wants is a medic who forgets us, doesn't check on our results or delays referring us to hospital.

With mindfulness I can see more clearly what drives me. As a process of introspection it has helped me to identify and take ownership of my role in the stress I experience. Like many of my patients, I tend to focus on what's making me feel worried or unhappy in my life, and try to work out how to change that: perhaps I need to alter my schedule, perhaps I should see more of my friends, perhaps I need a new job, and so on. These things may be true, perhaps, and I've contemplated them all at one time or another. But it's also true that my *perception* of the situation is contributing to how I feel. Mindfulness helps me notice my own contribution to stress and to work with it – not with criticism – but in an interested and accepting way. This allows me to deal more clearly with the reality of the situation, rather than being driven by automatic responses and looking to blame others for the way I feel.

Ed's Experience

I clearly remember the day a psychotherapist told me to 'observe my experience'. I took the bus back home and, putting her advice into practice, suddenly became aware that it was possible to look at the workings of my mind from an outsider's perspective. I could watch myself getting on the bus and walking up to the top deck, and then notice myself seeing all the people below on the street. I could watch my mind having thoughts about these events without necessarily being caught up in them. This was a revelation to me – my first conscious experience of 'meta-cognition'.

A year or two later, after some months of practising meditation, I was able to click into this mode more often. And the next time I became depressed, I was able to relate to the experience somewhat differently. Yes, I still felt in pain; yes, my mind was still racing; and yes, my thoughts were still spinning through the most negative scenarios possible. But I no longer had to be an active participant in all of that – I could disengage from the thoughts, emotions and body sensations, and just notice them – however unpleasant they seemed. This had the effect of reducing the sting of the depression as well as stopping me from adding fuel to its fire. Rather than agreeing with the thoughts that told me: 'This will never end' or 'I am totally useless,' I could let them all motor through my mind and see them as false perceptions rather than objective truths. I could come back down into my body, and even though this might mean relating with painful sensations, it also increased my sense of stillness, balance and wholeness, as I let go of thoughts that might otherwise carry me off into stress.

I won't pretend that mindfulness makes depression easy to cope with – it doesn't – but I do know that my own episodes have become shorter, less frequent and less painful since I've been practising. Just as a wound on the skin heals more quickly if you don't scratch it, so depression seems to pass more readily if I'm kind to myself rather than getting more irritated. It feels counterintuitive, but depression seems to ease if I can make friends with it.

· ·

CHAPTER 5

MINDFULNESS OF FEELINGS

When we create space to feel our feelings, it loosens the life-limiting bonds of addiction.

In Buddhist descriptions of the causes of suffering, it's our determination to grasp for pleasure and escape pain that makes us unhappy – by leading us into self-defeating behaviours that actually make our situation worse. The second noble truth calls this 'clinging' – these days, we often refer to it as addiction.

We're not just talking here about addiction to alcohol or drugs. For some of us it's working late to distract ourselves from loneliness; for others it's obsessive gym-going, perhaps to lessen anxiety about our ageing bodies. Some people get a buzz from the piece of chocolate cake they have with their coffee, or from speeding down the motorway or putting money on the horses. Maybe you're addicted to lying under the duvet for as long as you can each morning, or to getting the suntan that might make you more desirable to potential lovers? Or perhaps you are attached to zoning out in front of the TV, or having your tea made with just the right amount of milk?

It's not that going to the gym, having a nap, eating chocolate cake or drinking a beer are necessarily bad things to do. The problem comes when we engage in these activities compulsively, in a bid to manipulate our experience. Psychologist John Bradshaw's definition of addiction is 'a pathological relationship to any mood-altering experience that has life-damaging consequences'. According to this definition, we're addicted any time we repeat something that's supposed to make us better, but actually ends up hurting us.[1]

Let's take smoking as an example. Cigarettes provide a short-term relief from anxiety. The inhalation of nicotine into the body, the comfort of sucking on the filter, the relief of having something to do with the hands and mouth – all of these actions create small distractions from whatever is troubling the smoker, whether it's nerves before a job interview, the boredom of waiting at a bus stop or some nagging existential doubt ('Why am I here? Where is my life going?').

But the strategy doesn't work well in the long term. We can't escape our nervousness so easily – uncertainty and change are part of life. Cigarettes might temporarily distract us from it, but the costs are enormous. Smoking massively increases our risk of heart disease, emphysema, lung cancer and a whole range of other unpleasant illnesses. Each cigarette offers short-term relief from the discomforts of the moment, but it also hastens some of the things we get most frightened about – bringing illness and death ever closer. Despite all the warnings, one in four UK adults keeps on puffing, and 120,000 people die each year from tobacco-related diseases.[2]

Maybe you're not a smoker – perhaps you gave up long ago, or never started. That's great, but can you really say you have no addictive patterns that create a smokescreen from feelings? For some of us, it's alcohol – one in three men and one in five women regularly drinks more than the recommended limits, using booze to take the edge off emotions.[3] For others, it's food – around a quarter of us are obese,[4] and many more of us stuff down feelings by comfort-eating. Shopping can be addictive, too – we splurge on items we hope will be satisfying, but end up feeling empty once the thrill of buying has passed.

When we get a new coat, is it really because we need protection from the cold, or because its warmth is a substitute for what we really want, perhaps a hug from a friend or partner? When we sit engrossed in a computer game or watching TV for hours, is it because we really enjoy it, or so that we don't have to face our fear of going out and meeting new people, or our anger at a family member or work colleague? We can use almost any activity, any form of impulsive doing to distract our attention from painful feelings that are part and parcel of life. It could be sex, food, books, gossip or marijuana – as Pema Chödrön puts it: 'We use all kinds of things to escape – all addictions stem from this moment when we meet our edge and we just can't stand it.'[5]

Our strategies for avoiding feelings aren't always external ones – these patterns play out in our minds and bodies, too. We resist unpleasant emotions in the body the same way that we resist other kinds of physical pain – we contract and tighten in the area that gives us discomfort, or we retreat into our heads. In each case, the resisting, distracting and retreating has the unintended effect of perpetuating our distress, even as we are hoping to avoid it. And so we end up making ourselves more tense, more miserable.

We all want to be happy – it's just that the strategies we tend to employ keep us locked in cycles of discontent. When we keep resorting to them, we never learn more effective coping skills that might help us manage our emotions better.

So why don't we just stop it? If compulsive shopping drains our finances and brings us a house full of junk, why don't we restrict ourselves to what we really need, and spend our money on something that'll really make us feel good? Why do we so often choose to drink, smoke, spend, shout, binge, over-analyse or work obsessively when they have such damaging consequences?

THE ANSWER IS THREE-FOLD

First, we don't always see clearly what we're doing – unless we're aware that our addictive patterns are destructive, we'll have no reason to stop. Until the link between cigarettes and lung cancer was proven, there was far less awareness of the damage that tobacco could do to our health. People might have thought it was a dirty habit, but they didn't know it was going to kill them – and so a lot more people smoked.

It usually takes a heavy dose of awareness to convince us that we need to change our habits. Even though we know now about the dangers of smoking, people still find justifications to continue: 'I'll give up in a few years, before it does any real damage,' 'My granddad smoked and he lived till he was 90,' 'I'm a risk-taker – I don't care if I die young, as long as I've had fun.'

It's the same with our other addictions – we say we drink because we like a party (not because we feel anxious in social situations), or we buy the most expensive clothes because we're stylish, not because wearing designer labels gives us the confidence we lack. We'll do almost anything to avoid painful feelings. The Buddha said that we continue to get stuck in craving because of ignorance, or delusion. In Western psychological language, this is called denial.

Even when we're aware of what we're doing, it's not so easy to drop our defences. Though they may be storing up pain in the long run, our addictive behaviours can make us feel somewhat better – for a bit. Cigarettes might mask some anxiety when you're smoking, just as driving a fast car may help you feel more alive and powerful when you're hitting top speed on the motorway. When we let go of our habitual patterns, we're suddenly exposed to the very feelings of fear, sadness, emptiness or rage that we've been trying to avoid. And most of us have plenty of these – just as evolution geared us towards 'negative' thinking as a way of being alert to threats, so unpleasant emotions that prime us to react to danger are more common and insistent than pleasant emotions like joy. Releasing ourselves from addiction means having to face our anger, or our fear. Ouch. No thanks. The more stressed we are, the more insistent these emotions tend to be, and the more difficult it is to face them – therefore, the greater hold our addictions have on us. We're like lab rats taught to self-administer drugs – the more stressed the rodent, the more it'll use the substance to cope.[6]

We also keep doing what we've always done because that's what we're used to – it's the path of least resistance. We're creatures of habit, and if we've spent 30 years using coffee as our tool for waking up in the morning, stopping our caffeine fix is going to take work – it means retraining ourselves to behave in a new way. This is especially hard if we're using substances or processes that send our brain and body systems into withdrawal when we give them up. It's also difficult to stop if our addictions are socially acceptable – why should we cut down on shopping, drinking or rushing around if that's what everyone else is doing? The more our addictive behaviours are shared and reinforced by others – as they often are in a culture that promotes instant gratification – the harder it is to go against the grain.

But facing our feelings brings greater rewards than those offered by our addictions. It's true that when we stop acting compulsively, we open ourselves up to painful emotions, rather than closing them off. But in doing so we start to free ourselves from the hamster wheel of grasping and avoidance that doesn't bring us peace. Not only that, but we create space within to experience the vividness of life, including feelings of joy, love and connection that also get suppressed when we hide from pain.

By creating a gap where our addictive patterns used to be, we free up the whole of our emotional register. Instead of the deadness of addiction, we start to feel more present to our ever-changing bodily experience – the pleasure and the pain. Because we are opening ourselves up, our lives start to become richer. Only by letting go of our addictions – at least to some extent – can we really make contact with the wonder of our lives: the majesty of the sun at daybreak, the touch of a lover's skin, the beating of our own heart.

We can feel all of this in our bodies. Even so-called negative emotions may be useful – offering important information that can help us work with situations intuitively. Our anger or fear may be telling us we need to take ourselves away from harm or abuse – if we shut ourselves off from these feelings, we are more likely to get stuck in painful situations.

The Tibetan meditation master Chögyam Trungpa Rinpoche described our attempts to avoid feeling as like building a cocoon.[7] In this cocoon, covered with layers of thick psychic armour, we feel safe – well-defended from our emotional pain. But the cocoon also shuts out the light of life – we might feel less vulnerable inside our shell, but we also feel claustrophobic, dark and restricted.

Coming out of the cocoon doesn't mean acting out all our feelings. When we rage at someone, we might think we're very in touch with our anger, but that's not quite so.

Instead, it's more likely we're over-identified with it and, because we don't like it, we try to get rid of it as fast as we can, offloading it onto someone else. This too is self-defeating – by dumping our emotions on others, we create misery for everyone involved. People shout back or avoid our company, and we're left with more painful feelings to contend with, perhaps embarrassment and loneliness on top of our frustration.

EMERGING FROM OUR COCOON

Practising mindfulness can help us emerge from the cocoon. In meditation we don't resist our feelings, but neither do we identify with them. Instead, we practise bringing attention to them, and staying with them. Then we can start to see them more clearly, and increase our capacity for regulating them. We create space for working with difficult emotions wisely.

Mindfulness practice is an antidote to forces that keep our addictions in place. Instead of reaching for a cigarette, an explanation, a walnut whip or our wallets, we let go of clinging and actually look at what we've been trying to avoid. We notice our anger, and investigate whether it's really so intolerable that we must dump it on others? We notice our worry, and explore being friendly to it. We stay with our sadness rather than immediately trying to rationalize it, or push it away.

In this space of being, we naturally begin to develop greater freedom from our habits. We may even discover that emotions pass through us and dissolve, just like thoughts pass through the mind and dissolve. Sometimes all we need to do is actually feel the emotion that's calling for our attention, allowing its energy to move through us and evaporate.

GIVING YOUR EMOTIONS ROOM TO BREATHE

Staying with our emotions and letting them be as they are isn't easy. Our habits are woven into us, and we need real motivation to watch rather than react to strong feelings or urges. Perhaps this is why Chögyam Trungpa Rinpoche called this foundation 'mindfulness of effort' rather than 'mindfulness of feelings'. In making the effort to practise mindfulness – not a striving kind of effort, but a patient, gentle kind – our habitual pattern of walling-off can soften, and we can begin to experience the fullness of our emotional life. This means applying the same methods that we use to work with our breath, body sensations and thoughts – directly experiencing our feelings with curiosity and without buying into judgements of them. By taking the time to be with our emotions in this way, we start to gain a deeper understanding of how they operate.

We do this by bringing attention to the expression of feelings, in their physical location. A way to begin is to take the emotional temperature of your body as a whole: in this moment, are you experiencing joy, anger, sadness, fear or perhaps some combination of these? Whatever is there, can you investigate the tone of the experience: the sensations and energetic qualities, right where you are feeling them? Are you sensing a warmth in your chest, a tightening in your belly, a throbbing in your face? Or maybe there's a kind of blankness right now, no discernible emotional texture? Whatever you find, just notice it – not so much thinking about the emotion, as feeling its texture, its quality.

If you have judgements about whether it's a 'good' or 'bad' experience, just notice those, too. Be aware of any sense of aversion to what you are feeling, of wanting not to have this emotion, of wishing you were rid of it or, alternatively, of wanting to hold on to it, to grasp it tightly so it won't disappear. If you get caught up in thoughts about the emotion, simply notice that the mind has wandered and carefully return your attention to the feeling itself, resting with it, coming up close to it, accepting it, even if that feels unpleasant. What happens when you allow emotion to be as it is, holding it gently in awareness for a period of time? Does it shift in intensity? Remember that we aren't trying to change the feelings or create any particular experience, but simply discerning what's here, seeing it without manipulation, allowing it to be present. By coming into friendly contact with emotions in this way, embracing them as we might hold an upset child, we drop our sense of struggle. So while the experience might still be unpleasant, we are not aggravating it with resistance. This creates the potential for transforming the experience of suffering. We might start to feel that sadness, fear or anger are not problems in themselves, and that we don't have to try to banish them, but that we could even attend to them with the same warmth and affection that we might offer to so-called positive emotions. We might discover that when there's discomfort or pain, the awareness that 'knows' the experience is not itself in pain. In a wider, greater sense, we can remain in a state of wellbeing, even when we are going through the most profound turmoil.

FEELINGS, ADDICTION AND THE BRAIN

The part of our brain most commonly associated with emotions is called the *limbic system*. The limbic system evolved before other parts of the brain such as the prefrontal cortex, which is associated with 'higher' functions like reflection and self-awareness. The prefrontal cortex is proportionately larger in humans than in other animals – it's a mark of our relative sophistication.

When we're under stress, however, it's the more primitive limbic system that kicks in – it takes less than a quarter of a second to trigger feelings of fear or anger, provoking our knee-jerk 'fight or flight' reaction. Unfortunately, the more we face stress and react impulsively, the more sensitive the limbic system gets – the neurons in this, as in any other part of the brain, get strengthened with use. On a physiological level, this may be how our habitual patterns take root.

In the case of using an addictive substance, the substance triggers the brain's 'reward circuit', which then releases dopamine, a neurotransmitter that creates immediate feelings of pleasure. The user might feel good for a while, but there's also a come-down – the brain starts to make less of its own dopamine and, without the drug, a state of depression or anxiety can set in. Having stored the memory of the activity that seemed to 'solve' this problem, parts of the limbic system trigger urges and cravings to take the drug again. And so a habit starts to form. Other pleasure-seeking activities, such as eating and sex, can have a similar effect (over a longer time period) if we rely on them too much.

When we practise mindfulness, we are taking a more evolved approach – deliberately choosing to engage the prefrontal cortex to regulate our limbic system. That doesn't mean we won't experience unpleasant emotions, but we might not be so drawn to unhelpful reactions.

A study from Sara Lazar's laboratory showed that the amygdala, a key part of the limbic system sometimes called the brain's fear centre, actually became smaller in people who took a mindfulness course.[8] David Creswell and colleagues at UCLA also found that people who are more naturally mindful have less active amygdalas, while showing more activity in parts of the prefrontal cortex.[9] Another study by UCLA researchers discovered that meditators had more grey matter in areas of the brain linked to emotion-regulation.[10] Being mindful, it seems, offers a way of disengaging from the reactivity of the limbic system – helping us deal with situations in a more considered, reflective manner. This could explain why a study of 350 meditators found that those with more training had greater emotional intelligence, as well as lower stress levels and better mental health.[11]

To free ourselves of addictive patterns, we need alternative ways of working with feelings, urges and cravings. Mindfulness can help – by using our awareness to watch and stay present to our addictive desires and difficult emotions, we weaken the drive to react impulsively. We may still experience strong feelings – cravings to act in ways that are harmful – but the more we practise, the less likely we are to succumb to them. We can begin to rewire our brains away from addiction.

More and more studies are showing how both the MBSR and MBCT programmes can be useful in dealing with a wide range of challenging emotional states.[12] And over recent years, several new mindfulness-based programmes have been developed specifically to help with addictive patterns and relating to feelings.

Dialectical Behaviour Therapy (DBT) is a treatment that uses mindfulness practices to help treat borderline personality disorder. People with borderline personality disorder are often *overly* identified with their feelings – they can find it hard to contain emotions and, when these are painful, are easily triggered into acting out self-harming behaviours as an expression of their pain. When we live in thrall to our emotions, acting primarily on the basis of feeling, we will be easily tossed around by our anger, fear or sadness. Finding it difficult to contain ourselves, we'll tend to act irrationally. The mindfulness element of DBT is offered as a way of learning how not to be dominated by the 'emotional mind', and instead relate to feelings with a greater sense of awareness, a quality which is sometimes described as 'wise mind'.

Trials of DBT among women with borderline personality disorder have found it can lead to reduced self-harming and drug abuse, fewer suicide attempts and less frequent hospitalizations. DBT has also been shown to lower distress and anger levels, help people adjust better socially and improve their overall mental health.[13] Other mindfulness interventions have also been found useful in helping people manage their anger,[14] while in a group of university students, those classed as more mindful were also discovered to be less aggressive. More mindful people also have more awareness, understanding and acceptance of their emotions, and are less likely to react impulsively to them.[15]

Mindfulness is being used to help people with substance addictions, too. Until his recent death, Professor Alan Marlatt was Director of the Addictive Behaviours Research Center at the University of Washington, devoting his career to working with people who have problems with alcohol. His first brush with meditation was a personal one – he was encouraged to try it by his doctor when diagnosed with high blood pressure early in his career. Finding it helpful, Marlatt read up on some early studies that showed meditation could induce a 'relaxation response', and he thought it might help his patients. He carried out some research to back up this hunch, and found that meditation was as effective as regular exercise in reducing drinkers' alcohol consumption, and more effective than deep muscle relaxation and daily periods of quiet reading.[16]

Marlatt later pioneered the use of Cognitive Behavioural Therapy (CBT) to help prevent relapse among alcohol and drug users. The key element of relapse prevention is helping people develop coping skills to be used when stressful situations occur, to replace reliance on the addictive pattern. Inspired by Jon Kabat-Zinn and the developers of Mindfulness-Based Cognitive Therapy, Professor Marlatt's team felt that a mindfulness-based programme could make a real difference to people who struggled with alcohol. He and his team developed Mindfulness-Based Relapse Prevention (MBRP), which teaches meditation as a way of tolerating the inevitable urges that impel people to act on their addictions.

MBRP trains participants to interrupt the habit, watching and accepting cravings rather than being driven by them. This builds confidence that they can be withstood.

At the same time as Professor Marlatt was developing his course in Washington, London-based psychiatrist Dr Paramabandhu Groves had a similar idea. He'd already begun teaching Mindfulness-Based Cognitive Therapy to patients with depression, and quickly realized that virtually the same course could be taught to people who abuse substances. Dr Groves now runs MBRP courses as part of his day job with the NHS and at Breathing Space, a social enterprise which offers meditation to people in the East End of London.

CHARLIE'S EXPERIENCE

Charlie, 40, took a Mindfulness-based Relapse Prevention course six months after giving up alcohol. Without it, she suspects she may not have kept sober.

Charlie had been in a difficult relationship for 20 years; when it ended, her alcohol consumption sky-rocketed. 'I basically lost myself in drinking,' she remembers, 'self-medicating to deal with the emotions'. Eventually she was accepted into a detox programme, but, as with most substance users, she was plagued by negative thoughts and powerful emotions. 'I really struggled with stress and cravings, and especially my thinking processes,' she says. About six months into her treatment, the participants in her recovery programme were invited for an open day at Breathing Space, and Charlie went along with her social worker. 'I had a chat with one of the people there, and he recommended mindfulness. He said it might help me deal with my thoughts, and some of my overwhelming feelings.'

She was open to trying meditation – her mum used to practise it and had found it helpful. But because of her nervousness, the programme was not an easy ride for Charlie to begin with. 'Initially, I found it quite hard being around people I didn't know. But we all had something in common, so that made me feel safe.' As the course progressed, she started to relax.

The weeks passed, and she began to notice some 'dramatic' changes. 'I was able to focus on things more, and I became a lot more confident – more comfortable in my skin. I started to accept myself.' Learning how to practise working with thoughts and feelings in a mindful way was especially useful for her. 'The meditation helped me allow things to pass rather than thinking about them too much. Before, my mind was constantly working, which is typical of people suffering an addiction. I used to have problems sleeping, but now I'm able to go to sleep quite easily.'

Mindfulness also helped her cope with urges to drink. 'I can sit with cravings more easily,' she explains, 'staying with the feeling rather than avoiding it. Ultimately, the craving moves into another feeling.'

Two and a half years later, Charlie continues to use the techniques she learned on the course. 'I practise if my mind starts to race, or if I analyse and think too much. I bring myself into the moment and focus on what I'm doing. When I have a panicky feeling I can calm myself down and relax with the breathing – coming back into my body, asking how the ground feels under my feet or what emotion I'm having, rather than my mind wandering off in a negative way. You can do it when you're brushing your teeth, having a shower, or riding on the bus.'

Charlie's life is now back on track, but she says that, without mindfulness, 'I almost think I'd be drinking again.' She's training to be an alcohol and drug worker, and frequently recommends the MBRP course to others. 'Whenever I come across somebody who's struggling with anxiety, craving and negative thinking, I recommend mindfulness to them. It has helped me focus on what I want, and I'm more comfortable and real with myself. Mindfulness feels like something special that's a part of me.'

LETTING GO OF ADDICTION

There have been just a few studies of mindfulness-based relapse prevention so far, but the early evidence is encouraging. One trial followed a group of patients who took an MBRP course, and compared them with those in a standard drug and alcohol treatment programme. At the end of two months, those who'd learned mindfulness used substances less than half as often as those in the usual treatment group. After MBRP, the participants returned to the regular group and the differences disappeared, suggesting the importance of ongoing support for their practice.[17]

Mindfulness has also been used to help people give up cigarettes. James Davis and his colleagues at the University of Wisconsin offered a mindfulness-based stress reduction course to a group of smokers – when they experienced withdrawal symptoms such as irritability, sore throats or headaches, the group was encouraged to notice these in a non-judgemental, friendly and interested way. Although the participants were given a smoking quit date, they were encouraged not to focus too much on the 'goal' of stopping – instead, the course aimed to show them a more mindful approach to life. Of the 18 participants, 5 dropped out before the quit date. But of the remaining 13, only 3 had relapsed six weeks after the course. This compares to another group who were given counselling, of which just a third were still non-smokers after six weeks.[18]

Mindfulness is also being used to help treat some types of eating disorders. Jean Kristeller, Professor of Psychology at Indiana State University, has developed a programme called Mindfulness-Based Eating Awareness Training (MB-EAT). Just as people who are addicted to drink or drugs get cravings for their preferred substance, so people whose 'drug of choice' is food have a tendency to cope with stress by overeating, often bingeing on foods high in sugar or carbohydrates. Eating disorders are especially difficult addictions to handle because, unlike drugs or alcohol, it isn't possible to steer clear of temptation – we all need to eat, several times a day. People who are drawn to binge have to find a way to face their triggers, without succumbing to habitual patterns.

As well as sitting meditation, body scan and mindful movement exercises, MB-EAT incorporates a range of meditation practices designed to cultivate a more mindful relationship with food. This is a natural progression from the MBSR and MBCT programmes, in which the very first practice involves savouring a raisin mindfully. In a culture where we often wolf down meals on automatic pilot, the experience of mindful eating powerfully illustrates how rich and multi-layered our experience can be, when we pay attention to it.

PRACTICE: *The Raisin Exercise*

Perhaps you'd like to try the raisin exercise for yourself. The instructions are simple – take one raisin and place it in the palm of your hand. Offer your full attention to the object in front of you, exploring it as if you'd never seen such a thing before. Notice its weight and shape, its folds and hollows, really investigating how it looks from every angle. Try rolling it around in your hand, or between your fingers and thumb, or perhaps holding it up to the light – do the colours become more or less vivid depending on your vantage point? Tune in to the way the raisin feels as you hold it – do you notice any hardness, squidginess, stickiness or dryness?

Whenever your attention drifts away from the raisin – maybe into thoughts about what you're doing, memories of previous times you've eaten raisins or to something seemingly unrelated, just notice that the mind has wandered and return it to the raisin. Now, lift it up to your lips, but don't put it in your mouth yet. What happens? Is there an urge to gobble it? Do you automatically start producing saliva in anticipation? Place it under your nose for a while – what's the smell like?

Now put the raisin on the tongue, but see if you can resist any urge to bite into it – first exploring the sensation on the tongue and in different parts of the mouth, perhaps rolling it around, being curious about *this* experience. After a few moments, take a single bite, paying attention to the new sensations that arise – perhaps a burst of taste or juice. Also notice any judgements you find yourself making: is the taste pleasant or disappointing? Are you aware of a rush to swallow, or some irritation at doing the whole thing so slowly? Or maybe you're really grateful to be tasting the raisin in this mindful way? Whatever your reaction, just let that be in awareness as you continue to watch what happens, chewing the raisin, but perhaps more slowly than you usually might. Notice how it feels in your mouth as you work it into smaller and smaller parts. Finally, swallow the raisin, tracking its progress down through the throat and towards the stomach – do you sense the point at which you cease to feel the raisin as something separate from the body?

MINDFUL EATING

You can practise mindful eating with any piece of food – a satsuma, piece of chocolate, sandwich or full gourmet meal. The point isn't to munch everything at a snail's pace – it's to stay in contact with what's happening in the body, mind and feelings while you taste the food. Perhaps you could aim to eat one meal a week in this way, or just the first few mouthfuls of each meal. Can you pay particular attention to the sensations of hunger and fullness in the stomach? So many of us keep eating long after our bodies have had enough. With mindfulness, we can really feel how much food we want and need.

People often report that they start to appreciate food in a new way when they practise mindful eating. They become more present to the taste and textures of food, the way it looks and even the way it sounds as they crunch and swallow. Sometimes people report a sense of increased appreciation of where the food has come from and all the people who had a hand in getting it to them – perhaps farmers, drivers, shop staff and chefs.

In MB-EAT, mindfulness-of-food practices take centre stage. By learning to be mindful of thoughts and feelings as they eat, participants become more aware of the mental and emotional triggers that can spark a binge, and notice how those triggers naturally arise, change and evaporate without any need to act on them. This is the basis for appreciating food as a wholesome experience, rather than an addictive activity.

In a trial carried out by Jean Kristeller and her colleagues, an MB-EAT course was offered to 18 women with a diagnosis of binge-eating disorder – on average, they weighed 17 stone, and went on food binges more than four times a week.[19] By the end of the course, the average number of weekly binges had dropped to between one and two, while only four of the participants continued to show symptoms severe enough to be classed as binge-eating disorder. The women also reported feeling less depressed and anxious. Another study of more than 100 binge eaters found that those who practised mindfulness were able to reduce their binges from four times to once a week.[20]

ERIC'S EXPERIENCE

Eric, 28, is a successful businessman, and now weighs about 15 stone. But it wasn't always like that. He has a history of intense anxiety, and his means of escape from it was food – lots of it. At one point, his overeating resulted in him tipping the scales at more than twice his current weight.

'Obesity was an expression of my anxiety,' explains Eric. 'It was debilitating, and food had a sedating effect. It seemed to bring me down, in a good way – it made the anxiety manageable. After a long day at work I'd come in the door and had to eat sugary, starchy stuff to reach that point of calm. It was only some specific foods that would do it – if I had protein, like a steak with broccoli or something, I never felt that feeling I was looking for to calm me down. It was like a kind of sedation – an anaesthetic.'

Eric's anxiety dates back to his childhood. 'I didn't sleep from the time I can remember till the time I left home. I used to have nightmares of being kidnapped – I was constantly frightened.' Eating offered solace, but at a price. 'There was one pivotal moment... I was 17, walking up the stairs at school. It was only two flights, but when I got to the top my heart was racing – I weighed just over 30 stone at that point. I remember looking over the top of the stairs and thinking, "If you're going to live, then something has to change." When you're eating as much as I was, you're essentially destroying your body.'

Eric made a decision to lose weight – but his struggles weren't over. He tried both exercise and dieting, but nothing much changed. 'The way Western medicine focuses on obesity, it's all about eating less food and burning calories. That's certainly a component, but it didn't really deal with the main issue. For me, learning what foods are healthy, the behaviour modification and exercise were all secondary, because I was still plagued by anxiety, and that was what led me to eat in the first place. Dealing with that was the crucial part.'

But Eric couldn't deal with his anxiety while he still didn't understand how it operated, and why it led him to eat. 'The self-destruction was so subconscious that I didn't even notice what was happening,' he says. 'When I was shovelling food into my mouth I didn't really know what I was doing or why – I was eating before I even knew I wanted to eat!'

Eric was given a mindfulness CD by a friend's mother, and finally, things started to change. By practising mindfulness Eric feels he has grown 'a consciousness that didn't exist before, a sense of clarity'. This enabled him to notice what his 'addiction' to food was doing to him. Through practising, he has opened up a gap between the thoughts, emotions and body sensations triggering his compulsion, and the act of bingeing. He has been able to let go of his automatic, habitual reaction to fear and anxiety.

'Now eating comes as a result of making a decision rather than feeding a need,' he says. 'Before, there wasn't even an option. It was almost like taking in air – I felt like I needed to eat immediately or I wouldn't survive. It doesn't seem to be that way any more. Now eating is no longer just a reaction – I consciously consider everything that I put into my mouth. I get the urge, yes, but I don't act on it any more. I am able to manage the anxiety.'

For many of us, food is one of our most dangerous habits – dysfunctional eating patterns kill far more people than less socially acceptable addictions like heroin or crack cocaine. We eat not just when we're hungry, but when we're angry, lonely, tired or bored, filling ourselves up with calories that our bodies don't really need. Diabetes, high blood pressure, heart disease, arthritis and some types of cancer can all be brought on by eating too much of the wrong kinds of food.

We might not think of ourselves as having an eating disorder, but most people can relate to the same dysfunctional patterns that characterize conditions such as anorexia and bulimia – we pig out because we've had a bad day at work, or an argument, and then we feel guilty because we're worried about gaining weight. Consumed by shame, we may then punish ourselves with a stringent diet, which lasts until we have another bad day at work or another set of difficult feelings – at which point the cycle begins again.

Even when we're not bingeing or dieting, our eating habits tend to be mindless. Rather than paying attention to what our body needs, we fill it with junk. Rather than savouring the smell, taste and texture of what we put into our mouths, we shovel it in, perhaps simultaneously listening to the news, watching a programme on TV, replying to e-mails during an 'al desko' office lunch, or even just reading the cereal packet while we have our breakfast. When we eat like this, we're disconnecting from our experience. We're out of touch with our body and ignoring the signals it sends us about hunger and being full, unconsciously stuffing down feelings – perhaps loneliness, frustration, grief – in a way that distances us from life.

So we can all benefit from the practice of mindful eating – a middle way between the extremes of binge and diet. When we eat mindfully, we pay attention to how our body is before, during and after our meal ('Am I hungry? Does my body like or need this food? Have I had enough now?'). We become aware of our thoughts and all the messages they contain about diet (some may be positive: 'Mmm, I'm enjoying this chocolate much more than if I were rushing it,' while some may be negative: 'My mother always said I was a fat cow! I'm so self-indulgent.'), and we watch them all with kindly awareness. We notice our feelings as we begin to relate differently with food – does taking our meal slowly release feelings of anxiety or anger, or do we feel joyful at taking this time to really delve into the sensual pleasure of tasting? And we really pay attention to the food itself, appreciating it as one of the exquisite pleasures of living.

The scope is broad for mindfulness training to help us work with addiction and relate with emotion skilfully. It's already been shown that more mindful people exhibit healthier behaviours in relation to diet and exercise,[21] and there is even evidence that mindfulness might be able to help with our addiction to acquiring ever more possessions – research by Kirk Brown, Tim Kasser and colleagues found that people who are more mindful are less likely to want more than they have in financial terms.[22] This means they may be less likely to engage in the often fruitless search for happiness through acquiring extra wealth or material goods.

Whether our clinging is to heroin, the Internet, money, sex, tobacco, relationships, ice cream or success, when we use anything as a way of avoiding the experience of the moment, rather than engaging with it, we are setting ourselves up for greater stress in the long run. It may not always be easy to stay with our feelings, but when we do, we free ourselves up to live more flexibly and fully.

PRACTICE: *Mindfulness of Feelings – Riding the Waves of Emotion*

The experience of strong emotions can feel like a wave, crashing through our minds and bodies. Their power can seem awesome, but, like waves, emotions arise, peak and fall, and they can be surfed. By riding emotions – being with them – we sometimes discover that they dissolve more easily than if we give them more energy by ruminating about them, acting them out or trying to suppress them through addictive behaviours. This practice can help you ride the waves of emotion – and once you've developed your surfing skills, you can use it any time strong feelings, urges or cravings emerge.

STEP ONE

Begin by bringing awareness to the body as a whole. What emotional content are you experiencing right now? Where is it located in the body? Are the feelings strong, or more subtle? What's their energy like – a pulse, ripple, wave or throb? Perhaps you have a sense that you are taking your emotional temperature, receiving a reading of how you are feeling. If you can't identify a particular emotion at the moment, that's fine – just notice the absence of sensation. If you'd like to continue the practice, you might try visualizing a recent occasion when you were feeling a strong emotion, and pay attention to what happens in the body when you do this. Alternatively, you can come back to the practice when a strong feeling next arises.

STEP TWO

Now, if there's an area where the sensations are particularly intense, take your awareness to that part of the body. Place your attention on the sensation, just as you would the breath, or any other object of meditation. Your awareness is the surfboard you can use to ride the emotion. Rather than fighting the feeling, suppressing it or acting it out, see if you can just stay with it as it moves through the body. Be kind to the feeling, even if the feeling itself feels unkind.

STEP THREE

Notice how the sensation changes – or seems to stay the same – over time. Is it becoming more powerful, or softer? Is its location in the body changing? Is it starting to turn into another emotion? How is it not to act on the feeling, but just to carry on watching it, staying with it? Do you want to jump up and do something – phone a friend, eat something, go to work, rearrange your bedroom? Notice these urges and compulsions without judging them as bad or problematic. Experiment with not acting on them.

STEP FOUR

Notice any thoughts that arise as you stay with the feelings (perhaps 'I don't want to feel this,' or 'I want more of this'?). Perhaps there's a storyline connected to the feeling ('Why does she always leave her cup in the sink and not put it in the dishwasher?' 'I can't face another day in that office.' 'God, I need a drink!')? Let go of judging thoughts, and gently bring your attention back to the feeling in your body. If you find it helpful, you can label the emotion, perhaps saying to yourself: 'Oh, anger is here,' or 'Hello sadness,' or 'Having the urge to eat cake now.'

STEP FIVE

If the emotion is very intense, it's fine at any time to return to a more general sense of the body, or to practise mindfulness of breathing as a way to anchor your experience. If you decide to stay with the emotion, perhaps you could say silently to yourself: 'It's OK. This feeling is here – I don't need to push it away. I can be with it. I can feel it.' If you like, you can practise inviting the emotion into your body, as you might invite a guest into your house.

STEP SIX

As you come out of the formal practice, see if you can maintain some awareness of the emotion you've been riding. Perhaps check in with it at regular intervals – where in the body is it now? How has it changed since you were first aware of it? Has it been superseded by another emotion? As best you can, hold the feeling in awareness without identifying with it or distracting from it.

MINDFULNESS OF FEELINGS: SUGGESTIONS FOR PRACTICE

STARTING AFRESH

When we stay with our feelings in mindfulness, we are embedding new patterns, and this takes time – indeed, it's a lifelong process of becoming gradually more skilled in our practice. If you succumb to a craving, urge or feeling, it isn't a failure – just another opportunity to start afresh, to return to awareness, just as we can return to awareness when the mind wanders. Perhaps notice the effect that acting out the old pattern has, and compare it to what happens when you are able to stay present to your emotions. Be gentle with yourself – when things get tough, we all have the tendency to fall back into familiar habits.

DEALING WITH INCREASED SENSITIVITY

Just as some people report more thoughts when they start practising meditation, so others say that their feelings get more intense. This is probably because they're beginning to come into closer contact with experience. If your feelings appear to gather in strength when you practise, this may mean you are starting to become more alive to them. Remember that this will also allow you to experience and enjoy pleasant feelings more fully when they come along. If the emotions that arise in meditation feel overwhelming, it may be helpful to seek the support of an expert – a meditation instructor, psychologist or counsellor – who can guide you in this process.

USING DISTRACTIONS

Another way to develop our capacity to stay with feelings is to use whatever natural distractions arise when we practise. Can you resist the urge to scratch an itch, move your aching leg, roll your shoulders or get up and make a cup of tea? It doesn't have to become a torture session – just play with it and see if you can stay still a little longer than you usually would. If you decide to scratch the itch or move, can you do so mindfully, bringing awareness to the urge, the decision to respond to it and the action itself? In this way, responding to sensations can be a part of the practice, rather than a break from it.

NOT BEING ATTACHED TO HAPPINESS AND CALM

Sometimes in meditation we may experience strong feelings of joy, contentment, peace or love. These can be pleasant, but beware of getting attached to them – otherwise there's the risk of disappointment and frustration when they fade. Real happiness comes not from holding on to positive feelings, but from practising equanimity, even when our experience is unpleasant. Can you allow yourself to enjoy pleasant sensations without attaching to them, noticing your reactions when they (inevitably) change?

Jonty's Experience

I do a lot of work in the field of drug misuse, usually working with patients who have addictions to hard drugs such as crack cocaine or heroin. But actually, almost every consultation I participate in has change at its heart. As we have come to understand more and more about the causes of illness, there's an ever-greater responsibility on all of us to take care of our health. It helps to let go of those things that contribute to disease, such as smoking, and do more to help prevent ill-health by, for example, taking regular exercise and eating healthily. Unfortunately, these changes are notoriously difficult to make. There cannot be many of my patients, if any, who haven't heard or read about the risks associated with being overweight. And almost everyone I know who is overweight recognizes it as being something they need and want to change. They also know what they need to do to lose weight, yet somehow it's not that simple. Putting the theory into practice is hard.

Many of us feel stuck in a rut with our own unhealthy habits. I can't count the number of times I've tried to get into a regular routine of taking some exercise, eating more healthily, not snacking on the biscuits we keep in the practice reception or switching off the TV and picking up a book in the evening when I get home. But my unhealthy habits are so automatic and so comforting that, before I know it, I feel I'm back to square one. What mindfulness does is provide a very useful, practical bridge across this gap of ambivalence; it helps us remember our new intentions, without guilt, and motivates us to change because we want to, not because we should. It allows us to notice when we slip into self-defeating patterns of thinking or behaving, without criticism or judgement, and to see what's driving them, while riding out the impulse to act. It creates the space to make different decisions.

I now do some of those things I've mentioned (at least some of the time!) but I do them because I want to take care of my body and my mind. I've started to notice how I feel when I don't eat healthily or take regular exercise, how it affects my stress levels and my concentration. Mindfulness allows us to notice what we're doing to ourselves, how it really makes us feel, and then helps us to drop unhealthy habits by disengaging our autopilot for long enough to make different choices – based on caring for ourselves, rather than driven by guilt or insecurity.

. . . .

Ed's Experience

Giving up smoking was one of the best things I've ever done for myself – and mindfulness was a key factor. Having picked up the habit in my early teens, by my early thirties I was thoroughly sick of the smell, the cost, the coughing and the likely damage to my health. I'd tried giving up before, but it never lasted – I wasn't able to stay with the discomfort of withdrawal long enough for the new habit of non-smoking to take root. After a few years of practising meditation, however, I was ready to try again. It still wasn't easy – but this time I not only really had the intention to quit, but I'd also developed, somewhat, the ability to stay with experiences, even when they are uncomfortable. In the early days, each time I felt the craving to puff, I'd breathe in, place my attention on the feeling of desire and ride it through – staying in the moment rather than acting on the feeling it brought. Before long, the urge to smoke would subside and I could congratulate myself for not lighting up. As the weeks passed the waves of craving receded, and now, some six years later, I hardly ever feel a pang for nicotine.

I still have plenty of addictive tendencies – all too easily I can find myself eating, drinking, working, rushing or even reading books as a way of avoiding life, shutting myself off from painful emotions. But I always have a choice – a glass of wine can either be an escape or a fully enjoyed pleasure, depending on whether I can remember to engage with it mindfully or not. Can I sip slowly, savour the taste and appreciate the intoxication without over-indulging? Not always – but a great deal more often than before I started practising. Fortunately, mindfulness has also taught me to give up striving for perfection…

• •

CHAPTER 6

MINDFULNESS OF LIFE

Open your eyes and extend your awareness – bringing mindfulness into every situation helps us act more skilfully.

Meditation is often thought of as something we do to help ourselves – a way to improve our health and wellbeing. However, mindfulness can also be seen as having social implications – an important contribution to making the world a better place. That can seem like a strange idea to some people, especially those who see it as a somewhat self-indulgent act. It begs questions like: 'If you want to be kind and compassionate, why aren't you out helping the homeless, rather than sitting around "doing nothing"? How can sitting in silence and watching thoughts and feelings help other people – it's just navel-gazing, isn't it?'

It's true that the first three foundations of mindfulness *are* focused on learning how to relate more effectively with our internal experience. But there are good reasons for this: unless we first generate awareness of our habitual patterns, and cultivate the ability to work with them, we run the risk of continuing to act them out, perhaps unconsciously. We may keep doing harm, to ourselves and others, even when our intentions are good. Chögyam Trungpa Rinpoche memorably termed this tendency 'idiot compassion' – we think we're helping when we're actually making things worse. As the Dalai Lama puts it, creating outer peace is dependent on first creating inner peace. It's a bit like the advice we're given in aeroplane safety demonstrations – in an emergency, put on your own oxygen mask before trying to help those around you.

In the relatively structured environment of formal meditation, we learn to see our patterns of thinking and feeling, and how we are impulsively driven to act out those thoughts and feelings. We practise staying with our experience rather than being compelled by our need to 'do something'. But as meditators we don't have to be hermits, detached from the world. We are practising for living our lives: doing our jobs, being with family and friends, cultivating interests and developing our ability to live with wisdom and compassion. By choosing to dedicate some time to formal meditation, we are creating suitable conditions in which to train our minds and bodies, so that we can be present more often the rest of the time as well.

From there, we can begin to practise mindfulness in daily life. In this we are like a cyclist taking the stabilizers off their bike – having learned to maintain our balance in supportive conditions, we are more ready to expand our field of attention and try that same skill in more challenging circumstances. This is the essence of the fourth foundation of mindfulness: bringing awareness to all phenomena, which has sometimes been translated as 'mindfulness of life'. In this foundation we apply our attention to every aspect of our lives – we integrate our inner experience of body, mind and feelings with our outer experience of relationships, work and community. Having become more aware of what's going on inside us, we're more able to use that information to work wisely with what's going on around us.

So mindfulness doesn't mean moving around slowly all the time, or passing our days in meditative absorption. In the long term it doesn't even necessarily mean 'doing less'; to the degree that we can keep paying attention, we can do as much as our capacity for mindfulness allows. Top athletes are at their best when they pay highly focused attention to what they're doing – the movement of their bodies, a ball coming at them through the air – and combine this with a wider, open awareness of what's happening in the environment around them: the position of their teammates, the location of goalposts and so on. It's this combination of focus and openness that enables them to work with their whole situation effectively, acting in flow with what's going on around them. It's possible, and sometimes desirable, to do things quickly and decisively – if we can remain mindful, we're also likely to perform at the height of our game.

When we're mindful in our everyday lives, we're working with these two qualities of focused attention and open awareness, finding a middle way that allows us to notice what's happening inside us and around us at the same time. With attention, we're able to choose how and where to place our minds, not being swept about by every wind of thought, sensation or outside distraction, and with openness we can receive and process the information with a sense of equanimity. By paying attention to our lives in this 'particular way', as Jon Kabat-Zinn describes it, we can take our mindfulness into any situation and respond to it with care and warm-heartedness. Mindfulness practice won't give us fixed answers for how we should respond to a situation; instead it offers us a ground of intuitive understanding that enables us to make our own skilful decisions, based on all the information open to us.

THE IMPACT OF ATTENTION

In her book *Rapt: Attention and the Focused Life*, journalist Winifred Gallagher explores how choosing our objects of attention affects our lives. She describes how wellbeing comes not from being rich or famous, intelligent or good-looking, but mostly from being able to notice the things that we enjoy. It's a bit like the story of the man who owns two dogs that are prone to get into fights with one another. Asked which dog usually wins the scrap, the man replies: 'The one I feed!' So it is with our attention – if we pay attention to and cultivate the aspects of our lives that make us feel good, we will become happier. If, on the other hand, we feed and get stuck in our negativity, we are more likely to lose heart.

This doesn't mean we shut out negative experiences – stress reduction comes from using our wider awareness to see things as they are, and to hold difficult experiences kindly rather than pushing them away. But while we hold our experience in open awareness, we can then use our attention skills to notice which activities seem to bring contentment – relationships with the people around us, maybe, physical exercise, learning a new skill or helping others, all of which have been shown, through both experience and science, to cultivate wellbeing. By paying attention mindfully, we can become more attuned to what kind of activities lead us to greater wellbeing, and we can focus on them.

Researchers have carried out a range of experiments to test whether mindfulness practices can actually improve our attention skills. At Penn University, Amishi Jha found that after a course of mindfulness-based stress reduction, people who had never meditated before showed a distinct improvement in their ability to concentrate.[1] Jha also discovered that experienced meditators who took part in a one-month retreat were more alert afterwards. Meanwhile, Heleen Slagter, working with Richard Davidson at the University of Wisconsin, found that a three-month meditation programme improves people's ability to detect visual cues that most of us wouldn't notice. This suggests that, after practising intensively, we are likely to perceive more of what's going on in the world around us.[2]

Over at the University of Kentucky, Bruce O'Hara instructed a group of students to either meditate, sleep or watch television, before asking them to press a button when he flashed a light up on a screen. The students who had meditated reacted considerably faster, with those who had slept performing slowest.[3] And at UCLA, Eileen Luders and her team found that areas of the brain important for paying attention are larger in people who meditate compared to a set of control subjects with no meditation experience.[4]

This all suggests that by toning up our attention skills with mindfulness, we can choose more consciously what we want to focus on, rather than being so in thrall to our habitual patterns. By balancing this with the more open, accepting quality of awareness, our attempts to 'focus on the positive' are less likely to become grasping or aggressive – when our mind wanders away or tries to hold on too tightly, it's just another opportunity to practise gentleness and self-compassion, to come back into balance and make a fresh start.

TRY SOME AIMLESS WALKING

One way to practise this balance of focused attention and open awareness is by going for an 'aimless walk'. Aimless walking encourages us to let go of the 'get from A to B' goal-orientation that usually drives us when we are on the move, allowing us instead simply to pay attention to whatever's in our path. Just as we can watch our thoughts, feelings and bodily sensations without judging them, so during aimless walking we practise being curious about everything we encounter along our way.

To begin, just stand up and start walking in whatever direction seems to call you (provided, of course, it's a safe place for you to go). Notice any impulses to turn your walk into a planned journey, any attempt to get somewhere, speed up or fulfil a particular task – beyond simply being present to your experience of walking. If your mind wanders a lot, it can be helpful to place some of your attention on the soles of your feet as you walk for a while, feeling the rise and fall of the foot with each step and its contact with the ground. Once you feel somewhat grounded, allow your awareness to expand out more to the rest of your experience – sensations in other parts of the body, thoughts and emotions, as well as the sights and sounds around you. You may want to stop every now and again and bring your attention to a particular object you encounter, exploring it more closely with your eyes, or noticing any sound it makes.

When you let go of the 'doing' aspect of your relationship with the world, how does this change your experience? By placing your attention fully on a parked car, rather than rushing past it, do you notice elements that would otherwise have gone unseen? Scratches on the bodywork, reflections in windows, a broken windscreen wiper, personalized number plate, or parking ticket? Is it possible to find each of these interesting and curious, even though they might otherwise have seemed mundane, or have gone ignored? You can practise aimless walking in the city, in a park, in remote rural areas or at the beach – anywhere you have the freedom to take an ambient stroll. You can practise for ten minutes, half an hour or longer.

Aimless walking is, of course, another formal meditation practice. But once we have a flavour of this 'being' mode of relating to the world, we can start to integrate it with our daily life activities. Far from being an escape, mindfulness becomes a means for relating skilfully with any situation.

ACCEPTANCE AND COMMITMENT

This mindful attitude to working with everyday life is reflected in the name of a new psychological approach, Acceptance and Commitment Therapy (ACT). The acceptance part of ACT reflects the importance of the first three foundations of mindfulness. If we're to make wise decisions rather than automatically following skewed perceptions and unenlightened impulses, we need to check in with our bodies, thoughts and emotions. We can then practise accepting our experience when it's unpleasant or difficult, and minimize the amount of extra suffering we create in reaction to it.

If all we do is accept our experience, however, then nothing much changes. The second component of ACT is commitment – the willingness to engage in helpful behaviour. Having increased our awareness and practised accepting what we encounter, the action we take can then be guided by our basic intelligence, based on the sensory information we receive. We can touch in with our inherent wisdom, allowing ourselves to trust that making a deep connection with circumstances will enable us to act mindfully, rather than in a tight, striving kind of way, or in a manner that distracts us from what needs doing. We can see and feel more clearly what will lead to greater suffering, and what's likely to lead to contentment.

Imagine that you are faced with a difficult colleague at work. You feel that they're constantly criticizing you, putting down your abilities, minimizing your achievements and denting your confidence. How might such a situation affect you? Touch in with mindfulness of body, mind and feelings to get a sense of how you feel when you visualize this scenario. Is there a knot in your stomach, a boiling of the blood? What are your thoughts – do you find yourself believing the criticisms, or mentally attacking the colleague with put-downs of your own? Do you feel angry, frightened or helpless?

Now, having taken your internal temperature in this way, ask yourself: 'What's the best way for me to work with this situation?' The answer – or answers – that emerge will depend on your own personality, that of the critical colleague, your working environment, the attitude of your boss and many other variables. Whatever these are, by approaching the situation in a mindful way rather than reacting impulsively you stand a greater chance of making a good decision.

Mindfulness is acceptance *and* commitment, letting go *and* taking action. These are not the contradictory strategies they might sound – they reflect a potentially harmonious integration of the 'being' and 'doing' modes of living. Learning how to *be* actually makes what we *do* more effective – wise action starts to emerge more spontaneously as we set our intentions and drop our attempts to make things conform to preconceived ideas. Through this process, we are learning to dance with life.

MINDFULNESS FOR LIFE

What would it be like if we could be mindful when we're stuck in traffic, having an argument, enjoying a beautiful sunset, playing Scrabble, doing laundry, going for a jog, having dental work or sitting in a six-hour meeting? Could it actually enhance these situations for us, allowing us to connect with and deepen our experience rather than splashing around on the surface? Could this be the way to transform our lives, rather than always trying to make things different?

And could this also be the way to transform our world? Could mindfulness have an impact on our society that goes beyond the confines of 'self-help'? In fact, mindfulness takes us out of the limitations of self – by connecting us to a wider view, it shows us how we can fruitfully interrelate with others. This is true even if we're the only person in our community practising meditation – in which case we are helping others by seeing situations clearly, and being less prone to react impulsively when other people press our buttons. But when a group of people start to practise, it can make an even bigger difference to the energy of the environment – instead of everyone contributing their patterns to a set of automatic chain-reactions, there's the potential for a powerful, conscious change in the status quo, fuelled and supported by the growing awareness, resilience and skilful action of each meditator.

Human behaviour is contagious – when one person starts to manifest a more compassionate, courageous presence, it's more likely that those around them will pick up on the same energy.[5] We can't make others be mindful to conform to our dreams of harmony (besides, such an intention wouldn't be in the gentle spirit of the practice) – rather, we can magnetize curiosity through embodying the practice ourselves.

MINDFULNESS AT WORK

Mindfulness is already having an effect in many group environments. Let's take the world of work as an example: according to the UK Health and Safety Executive, four in five employees reports feeling 'very' or 'extremely' stressed in their job, and the cost of work-related stress to the UK has been estimated at £3.7 billion a year.[6] Long hours, demanding bosses, difficult projects, pressure to succeed, interpersonal problems with co-workers – the potential for stress in our jobs is enormous, and it affects most of us at some time or another.

It's the same in many countries, all over the world. At Transport for London (TfL), a company that employs over 20,000 people who work on the city's tube and bus network[7], stress-related illness was recently found to be one of the top health issues resulting in employees being off sick. As any of us who travel in big cities at rush hour know, commuting environments can be stressful places – perhaps this is especially true for those who work all day in them.

To address the issue, TfL started offering a six-week course to help employees who were struggling with stress. The course combines the teaching of mindfulness practices with cognitive behavioural therapy techniques. Among those employees who have taken the course, days off due to stress, depression and anxiety have fallen by more than 70 per cent over three years (absences for all health conditions were halved). Participants on the course reported improvements not just in their stress levels, but also their quality of life – 80 per cent said their relationships had got better, 79 per cent said they were more able to relax, and 53 per cent said they were happier in their jobs.

Emerald-Jane Turner, the trainer who developed the course, says that participants often report using the mindfulness practices in their personal as well as their professional lives. 'Participants learn that they have some control over their responses, even if they can't control the events themselves – like something a customer says to them, for example. And they often take the learning home with them – they'll say things like: "When I'm on the phone with my ex-wife, I can step back instead of having a go at her." The breakthroughs that people have are sometimes quite extraordinary.'

Mindfulness may be especially useful for business leaders, not just for stress management (three-quarters of executives say that stress affects their health, happiness and home life, as well as their work performance),[8] but also for promoting the kind of 'mindful leadership' that might permeate an entire organization. According to the business school INSEAD, access to meditation-based executive coaching programmes make it more likely that managers will act in a socially responsible way.[9]

Michael Chaskalson is a mindful workplace specialist who has run leadership training in companies such as KPMG, PricewaterhouseCoopers and Prudential, and he describes how mindfulness can help make work a more enjoyable and rewarding experience. 'By developing greater awareness, you can enjoy better relationships with your colleagues, be more able to renew yourself from stress, and develop your attention. You can't have too much mindfulness – whatever the problem is, if you're better able to work with the content of your mind, things will go better for you.'

It may go better not just for you, but for your colleagues and company, too – in a trial of acceptance and commitment therapy delivered in an organizational setting, participants not only enjoyed better mental health, but their ability to be creative also improved – perhaps as a result of being able to stand back from problems and view them from the 'bigger picture' perspective that mindfulness offers.[10] This means staying present to a problem when our temptation is to panic or close down, listening to the opinions of others before jumping in to prove ourselves right and others wrong, and cultivating the focus that helps us act clearly, calmly and decisively – all skills that are highly prized for effective teamwork and leadership. When we are present at work, just as in any other aspect of our lives, we are more open to possibility, attuned to ourselves and others, and poised for considered action. Indeed, another recent study suggested that people who meditate regularly make more rational decisions.[11]

With greater mindfulness, police officers might notice details of a case that would otherwise be missed; journalists might listen better to their interviewees, understand their own biases and create a more balanced and accurate account of a story; lorry drivers could use the road more safely as they pay greater attention to their vehicle, cargo and fellow motorists. Whatever job you do, practising mindfulness could help. Perhaps you have a sense of how it could help you in your work?

GOOGLING MEDITATION

Search engine giants like Google are just one of the increasing number of organizations that are offering meditation training to their employees. Over the last few years, Google has developed a mindfulness-based emotional intelligence training programme for staff at its California headquarters. The programme, called 'Search Inside Yourself', was inspired by Chade-Meng Tan, a Google executive who believes that more widespread meditation practice is key to a happier society. Google already operates what might be considered a mindful approach to office life – as well as working in a spacious, open environment, Google staff are encouraged to spend one day a week working on a self-generated project that interests them, in the expectation that free-flowing creativity will lead to innovation.

This attitude has been taken one step further by the Search Inside Yourself programme. The course presents meditation as a mental technology based on scientific principles – a way to exercise the mind just as physical exercise offers a workout for the body. As well as lectures from eminent speakers in the meditation field, there is practical training – six weekly two-hour meditation sessions, plus a one-day retreat. Participants are also offered tips on how to adopt a more contemplative approach to their jobs – how to listen more attentively to colleagues, for instance, or send mindful e-mails.

MINDFULNESS AND THE CARING PROFESSIONS

Greater mindfulness can be a wonderful healing balm in professional caring environments. By fostering an attentive, non-judgemental attitude, the practice can bring out our ability to listen and respond skilfully to those in distress. Those who work in the helping fields are often acutely aware of their need for tools that enable them to work effectively with clients and patients, and to handle the great pressure of their jobs. In a study conducted by Michael Krasner at the University of Rochester, a year-long mindfulness course for doctors was found to reduce burnout and exhaustion, and also increase the physicians' ability to empathize with their patients.[12] An earlier study by Dr Shauna Shapiro at the University of Arizona also found that an eight-week mindfulness course for medical students led to an increased ability to empathize with patients, as well as reducing the students' own stress and anxiety.[13] Empathy is crucial to a doctor's 'bedside manner' – not only does it make a big difference to patients' experience of the care they receive, but it may well affect their recovery prospects. Another study found that patients of psychotherapy interns who had been trained in mindfulness did better than patients of interns who had not received the training – evidence that the mindfulness of the healer rubs off on their patients.[14]

Technical and diagnostic skills are important in a health care context, but in the rush to fix a problem, or in the midst of bureaucracy and procedures to follow, the medicinal value of simply listening can sometimes be lost. Offering mindfulness training for professional carers could help them to be more present to those they look after, enabling them to relate more often in an inherently healing way. Mindfulness is simple and inexpensive to learn, so it might be an effective way to help manage the epidemic of stress-related illnesses that overwhelm our health care systems. It could save money, improve outcomes and enable people to make good use of their own inner healing resources. Most of us now understand that physical exercise is good for our wellbeing – how long will it be before meditation training is also a standard recommendation for optimizing health, and an integral part of the services offered to those who are suffering?

THE MINDFUL CHILD

We needn't wait until adulthood to teach people mindfulness skills. If we really want to cultivate the benefits that meditative disciplines can bring, we could prioritize the teaching of meditation in early life, before unhelpful habitual patterns become so ingrained. Several initiatives have already been developed to enable children to experience the fruits of mindfulness practice. In the UK, the Oxford Mindfulness Centre (OMC) and the Mindfulness in Schools programme have pioneered courses for children and teenagers that teach meditation in an innovative, engaging and age-appropriate way. The Mindfulness in Schools programme is called .b ('dot-bee'), referring to the content of text messages that pupils send each other, as a reminder to take a mindful pause in their day.

Mark Williams, the director of the OMC, says that young people are often open to being taught mindfulness – 'As soon as they try to meditate, they realize it's hard, so it's a challenge. They can become quite curious as to why it's so difficult to keep your mind focused.' In the US, the practices are taught to students through initiatives such as the Los Angeles-based InnerKids foundation, with research showing that even very young children with attention problems are more able to focus once they have been taught the techniques.

Trials of another adaptation of the eight-week mindfulness course – Mindfulness-Based Cognitive Therapy for Children (MBCT-C), has suggested it may significantly reduce problems such as anxiety and depression, as well as attention-span difficulties.[15] And controlled studies of the Hawn Foundation's MindUP programme, which teaches mindfulness as a core skill for social and emotional learning, has been shown to increase children's optimism and socially competent behaviours.[16] The programme is already being taught in more than a thousand US schools, aiming to help children reduce their stress and anxiety, develop their ability to pay attention and understand, observe and manage the connection between emotions, thoughts and behaviour.

It's estimated that up to 5 per cent of school-age children in England and Wales qualify for a diagnosis of Attention Deficit Hyperactivity Disorder (ADHD).[17] Wouldn't an approach that explicitly fosters the ability to pay attention be of use, not just to these children but for any students whose ability to learn is intimately related to their capacity to focus? A review of mindfulness-based interventions for children and adolescents by Christine Burke, published in the *Journal of Child and Family Studies*, suggests that it would – listing positive results with children from pre-school age upwards.[18]

Some researchers are attempting to intervene even earlier. Mark Williams has high hopes for mindfulness-based childbirth and parenting – together with California-based midwife Nancy Bardake, his centre is looking at how mindfulness can help pregnant women and their partners cope with the stresses of having children. Williams suggests that pregnancy classes offer a great opportunity for mindfulness training because 'when you're about to have a baby, it's the one time you'll accept class-based training without feeling pathologized – you turn up because you're scared. You want to get information and do the best by your child.' Based on the existing evidence for mindfulness interventions, Williams and his colleagues hope that mindfulness will help mothers-to-be deal with the fear and pain associated with childbirth, reduce the likelihood of postnatal depression and enable parents to form good bonds with their children. A controlled pilot study has already shown promise – reducing anxiety and depression in new mothers.[19]

Parents who are less stressed are also more likely to relate in a more open, caring and holding manner with their children, and are perhaps less likely to pass on unhelpful habits they learned during their own upbringing. By modelling mindfulness, parents offer the best chance a child can have for developing a flexible, friendly and resilient relationship with the world. Mindful parenting not only rewires the parents' brains, it can help wire the brains of children in a way that sets them up for a fulfilling life.

MINDFUL RELATIONSHIPS

Working, schooling, parenting – each is an aspect of life that requires some skill in relationships, and which appears to be enhanced by a mindful approach. From studies that rate people's mindfulness using questionnaires, and then asks them about their lives, we know that more mindful people enjoy more satisfying relationships, are better at communicating and are less troubled by conflict with their partners, as well as being less likely to think negatively of them when they've had an argument.[20] They also express themselves better in social situations, are more empathic and can identify and describe their feelings more accurately, as well as being less likely to experience social anxiety, or to be affected when people around them are distressed. There are correlations between mindfulness and 'emotional intelligence', the possession of which is linked to strong social skills, the ability to cooperate and to see things from another person's perspective. People who are more mindful are also less likely to react defensively when threatened.

Daniel Siegel, author of *The Mindful Brain*, presents mindfulness as 'a form of intrapersonal attunement' – in other words, it gives us the ability to understand our own minds.[21] And when we can see our own tendencies and perceptions more accurately, we also become more adept at understanding other people. From this vantage point we are more able to relate with compassion and empathy – we feel we know, at least to some extent, what those around us are going through. Similarly, when we are kind to ourselves, we are more likely to be kind to others. Because mindfulness means letting go of harsh judgement, we learn to refrain from seeing the people around us in terms of 'good' and 'bad' – we simply see them, without giving in to our tendency to think we are always right and they are always wrong (or vice versa). Rather than setting ourselves up to attack others, or to defend ourselves, we create a more open form of interpersonal communication – one based more on dialogue and a meeting of minds rather than a fight or a feud.

Mindfulness seems to enhance relationships in other ways, too. Because we each of us see the world in a unique way, to develop good relationships we have to be willing to understand how others perceive things differently. As if working with our own distorted view of reality isn't complicated enough, when we then add someone else's perception, which may be just as skewed as our own, there can be even more confusion. If we can take the time and space really to pay attention to what's going on for us as we listen to another person's perspective, we are more likely to refrain from automatically reacting to our own feelings of discomfort with impulsive attack or instinctive withdrawal. Staying present in this way can only increase the likelihood of compassionate communication.

So, perhaps, rather than getting angry with our partner for pulling away from us, we might remember that this is just their habitual response when they feel hurt or something is worrying them – we can make a mindful decision to approach them with extra love and care rather than pressure and frustration. Meanwhile, they may know that when anxious we get irritable, and can make the extra effort to come towards us, even when they feel like hiding.

In this way we can cut through interactions that might have become furious arguments or long stand-offs, and turn them instead into open conversations that bring us closer. We can move towards our loved ones, demonstrating that we have heard and acknowledged their perspective, and then work together to find a way forward which, as far as possible, meets our mutual needs. We can be more present to whatever's happening, in us, in others and in the environmental field – this intuitive sensing of the situation helps us respond to it more empathically.

This way of compassionate communication is at the heart of Mindfulness-Based Relationship Enhancement (MBRE), another adaptation of MBSR that aims to help couples improve their interaction with each other and deal more effectively with relationship stress. As well as the kinds of meditation exercises that form the core of all mindfulness-based approaches, MBRE places particular emphasis on mindful communication to develop empathy, trust and intimacy between participants, who attend as couples. According to research into the programme by James Carson at the University of North Carolina, MBRE improves people's relationship satisfaction, levels of closeness and acceptance of their partners, and decreases relationship distress.[22] Of course, this doesn't just apply to romantic relationships – any interpersonal connection can benefit from our being in a mindful mode. Practising mindfulness can enhance our friendships, our meetings with neighbours, our interactions in community groups, with shopkeepers, our children's schoolteachers and so on – any time we are called to engage with others, mindfulness can help those relationships flow more smoothly.

JANE'S EXPERIENCE

Jane, 52, is a company chief executive. She heard about mindfulness from a coach she was seeing at work – she had just taken on her first job as a CEO and she was finding it tough. 'I'd never run a business before so it was a steep learning curve,' she explains. 'When I took the job, the company was going bust. I hadn't realized what I had taken on and I was stressed out of my skull – I'm also a single parent – and I needed some support and a way to relax.'

As part of her company package, Jane had a small training budget that she was allowed to spend on anything she wanted. She decided to sign up for a course of Mindfulness-Based Cognitive Therapy. 'The course was fantastic, I loved it. I can take the messages, like "thoughts are not facts", and reinforce them in myself. I get really strongly that you don't have to go where your mind takes you. Instead of that whole conveyor belt of resentment and anger which I could get caught up in forever when I was younger, I can recognize it and listen to it but not go down that road.' She says that with mindfulness, she is now more able to manage the pressures of work. 'I am much calmer in the office, much more positive – even though my job can still be very stressful.'

Jane has also found mindfulness to be a powerful aid in her personal relationships. 'At first I thought that meditation might just calm me down. But then I started reading about mindfulness for depression and it became much bigger, much more useful. I was really depressed for five years after my partner left me with a young child. I went into therapy, and it feels like mindfulness has added to all that work. Since the course, my ex and I have become much better friends and been nicer to each other, so I think it helped in the very difficult healing of that relationship. Because I feel much better and can take care of myself, I can also help people around me.'

As someone whose parents died when she was young, the idea that mindfulness might be a way of self-parenting is also something that strikes a chord for Jane. 'One of my big patterns is feeling abandoned – especially if I haven't got someone to see or something to do. But I can go upstairs to meditate and that feeling of abandonment just disappears. It definitely feels like a way of parenting yourself, rather than getting someone else to do it for you. After the course I can say that I don't feel abandoned, I don't feel depressed and I'm managing things better. I feel like I can take care of myself, whereas before I often didn't want to.'

Jane doesn't think most people are aware of the importance of managing their minds, especially in frenetic big-city environments. 'People go to the gym, and they think about what they eat, but they don't often think: "I need to take care of my emotional health." Speaking as a city-dweller, I think we live in quite a hostile world. Mindfulness shows us how to take note of the positive – like when there's a friendly exchange in a shop or in the street. There's an exercise on the course where you practise taking note of pleasant experiences – I like that, deciding to notice the nice things in life.'

A MINDFUL WORLD

We can gradually expand the domain of our mindfulness outwards. We start by paying attention to our breathing, and then bring awareness to our bodies, our minds and our feelings. Gradually we can become more mindful of each aspect of our experience – relationships with the people around us, our work, community or home life. The potential for mindfulness to have an impact is limited only by the capacity of people to try it, embrace it and allow it to infuse their lives.

Mindfulness could transform our world, if enough people commit to it as a way of being. Imagine for a moment that not just you, but all your friends and family decided to start meditating. It wouldn't only be you who noticed how habitual tendencies get in the way of wellbeing, and how craving and grasping create more suffering. The people around you might slow down, start paying attention to their experience and begin to reap the benefits of greater awareness. They might also start to become more relaxed, and more discerning. Their discoveries could chime with your own insights, and you might start to feel supported rather than challenged by your environment. The energy of mindfulness could grow in power and, with increased confidence, you might feel more able, as a group, to be resilient in the face of cultural pressures to be speedy, aggressive and materialistic. You might all begin to feel less stressed. You might each get ill less often, and you might start to feel contented more of the time, more able to share the joys of the world with one another. You could revel in the miracle of being, together.

And now, imagine that the news about the benefits of mindfulness meditation spread much, much further. Imagine if instruction in mindfulness were available to every patient, with any health condition. Imagine that instead of telling us about the latest celebrity gossip, the latest car or the latest diet, newspapers and magazines chose what stories to cover based not on their capacity for appealing to our impulses of greed, fear or anger, but because they might truly inform us about the state of our world, and help awaken our awareness and compassion. Imagine that instead of pressuring us to work harder and faster, employers encouraged their workers to take time out each day to meditate, in the knowledge that real productivity comes from a calmer, clear-minded and energetic staff.

Imagine the possibilities for peace if mindfulness were taught in every primary and secondary school, so that instead of just learning how to pass exams and reach targets, children discovered from an early age how to 'be', embedding their learning in a framework of greater compassion, creativity and contemplative awareness. And imagine, just imagine, if instead of shouting about how useless their opponents are, politicians sat mindfully in meditation for ten minutes before each session of Parliament or Congress – pausing to disengage their egos and notice how their own unhelpful patterns of thought and feelings can drive their decisions. Could this start to shift the process of government away from defence and confrontation, and towards collaboration and cooperation?

Can you imagine a mindful approach to climate and environmental change, where governments were really prepared to be aware of, and choose to forego, short-term self-interest in order to meet our planetary crises in a way that will benefit everyone? Perhaps they might draw on the research that shows that mindful people are engaged in more positive environmental behaviours and have smaller carbon footprints.[23] Imagine, finally, what it would be like if the principles and practices of mindfulness underwrote our lives and our culture, a basis from which we could work towards creating the happy world that we all want, but which we seem to find so hard to manifest.

It certainly won't happen overnight. Mindfulness is a quality to cultivate, not a quick fix to hanker for – seeing meditation as a miracle cure would be to fall further into the speedy, solution-grabbing trap we so often get snared in. Nevertheless, if enough people commit to it, then gradually, over time, we could start to enjoy living in a world that embodies mindfulness. Such a world might be more insightful, less distracted and less reactive, with each practitioner's ever-developing awareness, resilience and discernment contributing to the whole and benefiting from it.

Global problems seem insoluble because of their magnitude, but at their root they're created and sustained by the same automatic, mindless patterns of thinking, feeling and behaving that motivate us as individuals and which can start to be understood and worked with in mindfulness practice. Across the world, quietly and steadily, there are a growing number of meditators in every field of life – mindful lawyers, police officers, teachers, doctors, business leaders, parents, politicians, economists, sports coaches, humanitarian workers and environmental campaigners – all of whom are using their practice as a ground for sharing the gift of presence with others.

In a world overrun by words and activity, planting seeds of mindfulness in this way will probably be more helpful than a host of fine-sounding plans or pledges. We can't 'impose' mindfulness from above, but we can invite everyone, including those in positions of influence, to explore the practice of meditation for themselves, to investigate whether it's helpful for them and, if it is, to create favourable conditions for it to spread, with space and resources made available in a range of community settings. Evidence from the burgeoning science of mindfulness may encourage sceptics to give it a try – if it works for them, perhaps they'll also help the practice to flower, as has already begun to happen. A simple way to start might be to allow a pause for meditation before business meetings, family meals, school assemblies or the day's proceedings at political conferences, open to anyone interested in taking part.

Thousands of years of experience and several decades of research show that, wherever there is more mindfulness, there is a greater possibility for compassion, wisdom and wellbeing to flourish.

This is why *The Mindful Manifesto* isn't just about self-help. Helping ourselves isn't enough – we aren't isolated entities, and when the world continues to push us in the direction of mindlessness, it's much harder to keep from falling into old habits. But if we can be more mindful in our own lives, and by our example inspire others to do the same, we set in motion a virtuous cycle, countering the vicious circle of speed and distraction that causes so much stress.

This is the essence of mindfulness of life – a natural expansion from practices centred on the body and mind of the individual, into a wider way of being that takes into account the interdependence and connection that binds us all together, and based on the realization that helping ourselves means helping others. Far from being self-indulgent, practising mindfulness is one of the most community-centred things we can do.

PRACTICE: *Mini-meditation for Daily Life*

As our practice develops, we may find we can approach more and more life situations with mindfulness. One of the greatest challenges here is to *remember* to be mindful – just as in formal practice, our awareness drifts away from the object of meditation again and again, so we are prone to forget to pay attention when we get into the swing of our lives. However, just as we can come back to the breath or the body when this happens in formal practice, in mindfulness of life we can acknowledge what's happened, return our attention to the situation we're facing and gently bring mindfulness into our way of being once more.

A tool you can use to practise this is the following mini-meditation, which takes you through each of the four foundations of mindfulness in turn – body, mind, feelings, and life. Allow some time for each step in turn (the whole thing could take anywhere from 30 seconds to 5 minutes or longer). It can be practised at your desk, on a train or bus, or in a supermarket queue – though it's not a good idea when you're driving or otherwise need your attention to be focused more externally.

At first it may be good to practise this at set times, perhaps several times a day, so you can get used to coming into awareness in the middle of daily life (you could set the alarm on your phone to remind you). You can also use it when you're faced with a particularly challenging situation, those times when we're more likely to fall back onto automatic pilot. It can help ground us in awareness, creating space from which we can choose to respond more skilfully.

STEP ONE

Take a relaxed, upright, dignified posture. Whether standing or sitting, cultivate a sense of being confident, present and awake. Close your eyes or leave them open, whatever works best for where you are now. Place your attention on your breathing. Notice the rise and fall of the chest and abdomen as you inhale and exhale. Connect with the breath as it moves in and out. Allow your mind to ride the breath, using it as an anchor to steady and settle your attention.

STEP TWO

Expand the awareness to what's happening in the body. Become aware of the whole body – and any sensations you may be experiencing right now. Just notice the bodily sensations rather than judging them, trying to hold on to them or pushing them away. If there's an area of more intense sensation, perhaps experiment with breathing into it on the in-breath, and having a sense of softening on the out-breath.

STEP THREE
Now, shift your attention to thoughts. Notice what's going through your mind – watch the thoughts as they come into awareness, pass through and fall away. Rather than attaching to or judging thoughts, practise accepting them as they are. Be curious about your experience and kind to yourself as you observe it. 'Aha, this is what my mind is doing right now.'

STEP FOUR
Turn your attention to the emotions. Are you feeling joy, sadness, anger, fear – or some combination of these? How are the feelings expressing themselves in the body? Where do you feel them? Are the sensations changing, or staying the same? Notice any tendency to create a mental storyline around them and, as best you can, come back to the direct experience of sensing.

STEP FIVE
Expand your awareness to take in the whole of your experience, including the environment. What can you see, hear, smell? How are your body, mind and feelings interacting with your life in this moment – the physical space you're in, the people nearby, any activity that's happening around you?

STEP SIX
As you come out of this mini-meditation, ask yourself, 'What's the most skilful thing for me to do now?' Try to be

genuine and listen to the response that comes from your heart. Allow your inherent wisdom to guide you, remaining in a mindful mode of being, as best you can, as you move through the rest of your day.

TIPS FOR MAINTAINING MINDFULNESS OF LIFE

Here are a few more suggestions for making your experience of everyday life more mindful…

TRAIN WITH EVERYDAY ACTIVITIES

A good way of integrating mindfulness into daily life is to practise while engaging in activities you might usually plough through on autopilot. Make a conscious attempt to stay present as you go through your daily routine: showering, getting dressed, driving to and from work, washing the dishes, exercising or vacuuming. You might find that paying attention to these everyday activities can radically change the way you experience them. Mindfully washing the dishes can turn a humdrum task into a vivid sensory experience (noticing the softness of the soap suds on your hands, appreciating the change from dirty to clean plates, experiencing the feeling of a job done well). Notice when you lose touch with your breath and your body, and practise bringing yourself back each time.

USE DIFFICULT SITUATIONS AS A MINDFUL CHALLENGE

It can be tempting to think that some circumstances are just too difficult for mindfulness – it's too noisy, too chaotic, too overwhelming, too painful. But no matter how hard the situation, is it likely to be more or less difficult if we are mindful or mindless? The important thing is to stay with the practice and not judge ourselves for 'failing' – indeed, our practice is a success simply by us remembering to engage in it. We do the best we can, and congratulate ourselves for that.

DEVELOP MINDFULNESS CUES
Traditionally, gongs and bells signal the start of a meditation session – can you turn the sounds of modern life into your reminders to be mindful? As best you can, get into the habit of noticing your breathing, body sensations, thoughts and emotions when your phone rings, or you hear the sound of a car, or you switch your computer on, or your wake-up alarm goes off in the morning. If you are rushing, use these cues to slow down enough to bring you into the moment.

PRACTISING MINDFUL COMMUNICATION
As best you can, listen attentively to others when they're speaking to you. Be aware also of how your body feels as you listen. Notice any resisting, tensing or rushing to control the conversation – can you stay present to yourself and the other person, creating space for a response that comes from the body, and not just from the head?

KEEP COMING BACK TO FORMAL PRACTICE
No matter how skilful we become, it's important to return again and again to the more structured practices, if possible reserving a portion of each day for them. Just as we need to keep exercising if we want to stay fit, so maintaining a formal meditation practice seems to help us hone our mindfulness. Don't beat yourself up if you fall out of practice for a while – just notice it and see if you can make a fresh start, without self-criticism.

Jonty's Experience

Doctors are very lucky, and don't let anyone tell you otherwise. We have one of the most fulfilling jobs it's possible to have, and yet a quarter plan to retire early – of these, a third cite stress as the reason. I've only been in general practice for just over ten years and I love it, but I've no doubt that the pressures it places me under are significant. Attending to people is hard work. Sometimes we don't appreciate just how generous our friends and family are being when they simply listen to us. Truly offering our attention to someone else is demanding – staying with them, listening not just to what they're saying but also what they *aren't* saying, and then trying to help them with whatever difficulty they're dealing with is a pretty big task – particularly if you're doing that for 30–40 people a day. If you then add the usual demands of running a business, looking after staff, maintaining the premises and all this while constant change is imposed from above, you can see that the pressures are high – particularly if, like me, you don't deal well with uncertainty.

I've no doubt that my need for perfection and relative rigidity make coping with these demands more difficult. Like many doctors, I like to solve problems – whether they are my patients' or my own. Like a dog with a bone, I find it very difficult to let go of whatever's bothering me. My shower in the morning is usually spent ruminating over issues at work, and I am renowned for staying late at the practice, trying to make sure that I've finished all my jobs for the day. While this may not sound like much fun, in and of itself it may not be a huge problem. But, of course, it doesn't stop there. My drive for perfection extends to my expectations of others, leading to frustration and criticism which can potentially damage my relationships with friends, family, work colleagues and even patients.

At work, mindfulness helps me not only attend to my patients in a more genuine way but also to notice how my coping mechanisms contribute to my own stress and that of the people around me. Gradually I've become more aware of the ripples I create in my life, both internal and external. While change isn't easy, at least by noticing how I contribute to this stress I give myself the chance to do things differently.

. . . .

Ed's Experience

There's a long tradition of hermit meditators – people who go off and spend long periods of time practising on their own. It's considered a noble thing to do – you're working on your mind so you can develop greater compassion and wisdom, rather than polluting the world with your confusion. However, it's also sometimes said that enlightenment can only come when you commit to helping others. I have at times used meditation as a bit of an escape from life – how luxurious to spend time on my own, in the quiet, paying attention to my breath rather than dealing with the chaos of the outside world. But I also know that this isn't really what meditation is about, and that much of the joy of life comes from relating with others – my extrovert side loves to be around people.

So while being mindful in relationships is a challenge for me, it's a very worthwhile one. It means noticing the tendency to want always to be right and my fear of being criticized, and allowing myself to stay open when the habitual tendency is to shut off. I've found that my relationships work better when I'm willing to listen to the other person's point of view, and not treat it so much as a threat. I'm much more aware these days of my mind's 'negativity bias' – its pattern of interpreting people's reactions in a way that's most threatening or fearful, and I'm more often able to remind myself that my perspective may not be the whole truth. Meditation practice has helped me allow more space in my body, my mind, my life. Even though I often revert to old patterns of tightening and resisting, there's the potential for returning to the open-heartedness of mindfulness in each moment. I practise checking in with myself as often as I remember, knowing from experience that doing so enables me to choose a way that is helpful to myself and those around me. It's a work in progress, an ongoing journey of acceptance and commitment. Realizing that offers yet another opportunity to be gentle with myself.

• •

CHAPTER 7

THE MINDFUL
MANIFESTO

How does it feel to 'be' now? You could try the exercise from Chapter 1 again – putting this book down and letting go into whatever arises. You may experience similar states of mind, body and feelings as before, but if you've been practising mindfulness, perhaps you might be starting to relate to them a little differently? Maybe there's a sense of not being so identified with your experience, of noticing it with a touch more gentleness, a touch more compassion, a touch less criticism? Perhaps you're able to stay with what happens a little longer, without reacting immediately and impulsively? Maybe you can even see some possible ways forward in your life, based on making wise decisions from a position of greater clarity and strength.

A WAY OF BEING

Experiments by Norman Farb at the University of Toronto seem to confirm that mindfulness can help us relate to life more flexibly, enhancing our capacity for being.[1] Using fMRI scanning techniques, Farb and his colleagues identified two networks in the brain, each activated by a different way of relating to the world. One network seems to drive the 'doing' mode – the part of us that is led by narratives and concepts. It triggers areas of the brain such as the medial prefrontal cortex and the hippocampus, and appears to become active when we're spinning stories about our lives, thinking through plans about the future, or ruminating about the past.

The other mode is more experiential, activated when we pay attention to the feeling of things as they are – more of a 'being' mode. When we operate in this way, other parts of the brain seem to become active, such as the insula, which is implicated in the experience of bodily sensations, and the anterior cingulate cortex, which is known to be important in regulating attention. Farb and his colleagues found that people who've learned to practise mindfulness have a greater ability to shift consciously between these two networks, whereas people who have not received meditation training are more likely to default automatically into the 'doing' mode. With mindfulness, then, we have greater choice over which mode we use to relate with the world – we can train ourselves to be, as well as to do.

Mindfulness is a simple, feasible and powerful way to approach life. There is no great outlay of expense or external resources required, and neither is there a particular agenda to follow, beyond the instruction to pay attention, be present and make decisions based on an innate wisdom we discover through the practice. Whether it's a physical or mental health challenge, a compulsive behaviour, a relationship problem, a work dilemma or a pervasive sense of alienation, meeting the situation in a mindful way seems to help.

As we deepen our practice, we might see more often how our craving for pleasure causes pain, and how our attempts to resist or escape suffering make it greater. We may no longer be so in thrall to the conditioning we received when we were growing up, or so easily give in to the social and cultural pressures to speed up and follow the herd, doing things that aren't good for us or for others. We might start to choose more consciously to engage in action that brings about genuine contentment. We might find ourselves spending less time living in our heads and more in our bodies, having realized we can't solve the problems of a busy mind with a busy mind. We might find more room to breathe, and be less prone to be dominated by small-minded concerns. We might enjoy the delights and beauty of the world a little more, perhaps without becoming so attached to them. We might be more able to accept and ride with the inevitable ups and downs of human existence, so life becomes less of an insult and more of a joy.

Great teachers and philosophers throughout history have suggested that these are the fruits of mindfulness practice. It's wonderful that the scientific understanding of mindfulness is now confirming this view. Misconceptions about meditation – that it's an escape from life, an ineffectual new-age indulgence, or something religious, foreign or weird – are much rarer today, especially in areas such as psychology and medicine. We have evidence borne of the scientific method to thank for that.

However, deep understanding cannot come through scientific evidence alone – for that, we need to embark on the kind of personal journey undertaken by every meditator who has ever started out on the path of awareness and insight, meeting the joys and challenges of practice through our own first-hand experience.

Scientific research can sometimes give the impression that mindfulness 'works' – that all we have to do is turn up to a course and our stress will be reduced, our pain relieved, our relationships improved and so on. Of course, all these things do happen, and the studies can be a useful inspiration to practise, but they can also lead to the trap of expecting an easy, clean solution. As soon as we begin to expect certain results, we are starting to close down the window of possibility that makes mindfulness so alive, falling instead into a goal-seeking, striving, fixating mode that can actually sabotage our practice.

Mindfulness is a means of connecting with reality in a deeply felt, somatic way that can't easily be expressed through scientific data, which necessarily presents evidence in a detached, objective, conceptual way. The experience of mindfulness is richer, messier and more subjective than that – everyone's experience is different because we all have different bodies, minds and life situations. We make ourselves willing to see what we see and feel what we feel – to touch in with our hearts. In so doing, we are granted access to a treasure of ever-unfolding moments, a kaleidoscope of changing sensations that are uniquely ours. Promises like better concentration, stress reduction or prevention of depressive relapse barely hint at the magic that could be unlocked.

There are no guarantees – meditation practice can be challenging, and often unfolds in ways we don't expect. When we come into contact with the present moment, we may experience times of great physical pain, strong emotions and awareness of truths that are difficult to face. At the same time, meditators who report such experiences sometimes say they are accompanied by, or lead to, a sense of release, inner ease or even joy. When transformation comes, people often say it isn't what they expected.

If we cling to a desired result – whether it's lower anxiety, better relationships or world peace – we may miss out not only on the outcome we're seeking, but the fascinating journey along the way. We're also setting ourselves up for disappointment when we find ourselves falling back into old patterns, or have a difficult time – all of which is likely to happen from time to time. The risk then is that we feel we've failed and give up, rather than seeing each distraction as a part of the path, another opportunity to practise coming back into awareness. So rather than trying to make things better, can we cultivate peace with who we are, where we are, right now? Curiously, when we let go into the present moment like this, things often do seem to get easier.

There's an old Zen story about a student, eager to attain enlightenment. In an interview with his teacher, he asks how long it will take. 'Ten years', comes the master's reply. The student isn't satisfied with this answer, and asks: 'How about if I practise really, really hard? How long will it take then?' His teacher thinks for a while and then responds: 'Twenty years.'

Of course, this tale isn't saying we shouldn't apply effort – we can set intentions and create positive conditions for our practice to bear fruit, and keep returning to mindfulness again and again when our attention wanders. But we can't force change, even positive change. Trying to do so tends to create more of the striving and aggression we're working to let go of. Mindfulness isn't so much a tool for self-improvement or self-control as a process of self-letting go: a deep dis-assembling from which a different way of being can emerge.

So long as we're alive, we can always come back to our breath and start again. This requires courage. If you're riding a horse you don't have to be brave to stay in the saddle; it's the getting back up when you've fallen off that takes fortitude. In meditation and in life, we can keep letting go and coming back, letting go and coming back, letting go and coming back…

Mindfulness is a synchronization of being and doing, a means of coming into flow with life which emerges from paying heartfelt attention to each aspect of our lives. If we know that fundamentally there's nothing to fix, and that our only job is to uncover and be who we really are, then no great plans of action are needed. When we touch in to our wise mind and body, we're already doing enough – the choices we need to make will become clear as we attune to our experience. The practice of mindfulness connects us with the heart of experience, so we can manifest more fully and more compassionately in our lives. As such, it's one of the greatest gifts we can offer, to ourselves and to the world.

FURTHER RESOURCES

In *The Mindful Manifesto*, our intention has been to give you a taste of meditation – where it comes from, how to practise it and what the benefits might be. If you're interested in exploring further, there are plenty of resources to investigate, and we've listed a few books and websites below that you might want to check out.

If you find yourself inspired to practise, we strongly recommend that you also seek out a teacher and a supportive community. The work of meditation can be challenging, so it can be enormously helpful to receive ongoing guidance and support. Fortunately, as mindfulness becomes more mainstream there are an increasing number of high-quality courses being offered across the world. In some places you may be able to access them via your doctor or other health practitioner – it may also be worth Googling 'mindfulness' and your region to see what is available near you. If you're attracted to the Buddhist tradition, there are Buddhist meditation groups and centres in most areas – the courses they offer are often inexpensive (or free).

THE MINDFUL MANIFESTO ONLINE

Please do come and visit our website at www. themindfulmanifesto.com. Here you can order or download guided audio versions of the practices described in this book, as well as sign up for our newsletter, and find out about mindfulness courses that we offer. For those who can't visit us in person, we offer some online and telephone distance-learning options. We also have a Facebook page, where we post news and views, and Ed regularly posts updates and shares links from his Mindful Manifesto (@ edhalliwell) Twitter account.

OTHER WEBSITES

www.mindful.org
Excellent online magazine site, featuring mindfulness news and features from around the world. Ed writes a regular blog for the site, called 'The Examined Life'.

www.mindfulnesssussex.co.uk and www. mindfulnesslondon.co.uk
Mindfulness Sussex and Mindfulness London offer group and one-to-one mindfulness courses led by Ed Halliwell.

www.mindfulnessretreats.co.uk
Residential UK-based mindfulness retreats, led by Ed Halliwell and other experienced teachers.

www.bemindfulonline.com
A four-week online mindfulness course, co-taught by Ed, which was developed as part of the UK Mental Health

Foundation's 'Be Mindful' campaign.

www.shambhala.org
An international community of meditation centres, led by
Buddhist teacher Sakyong Mipham Rinpoche.

OTHER BOOKS

When Things Fall Apart: Heart Advice for Difficult Times,
Pema Chödrön (Shambhala Publications, 1997)

The Wisdom of No Escape and the Path of Loving-Kindness,
Pema Chödrön (Shambhala Publications, 1991)

*Wherever You Go, There You Are: Mindfulness Meditation
for Everyday Life,* Jon Kabat-Zinn (Hyperion Books, 1994)

*A Path with Heart: The Classic Guide Through the Perils and
Promises of Spiritual Life,* Jack Kornfield (Rider, 1993)

Fully Present: The Science, Art and Practice of Mindfulness,
Susan Smalley and Diana Winston (Da Capo, 2010)

Shambhala: The Sacred Path of the Warrior, Chögyam
Trungpa (Shambhala Publications, 1984)

*The Mindful Way Through Depression: Freeing Yourself from
Chronic Unhappiness*, Mark Williams, John Teasdale, Zindel
Segal, Jon Kabat-Zinn (Guilford Press, 2007)

REFERENCES

CHAPTER 1

1. Mental Health Foundation (2009), 'In the face of fear: how fear and anxiety affect our health and society, and what we can do about it', at http://www.mentalhealth. org.uk/campaigns/mental-health-action-week-2009/in-the-face-of-fear

2. R Ramesh (2010), 'More money, less happy: Europe's wellbeing falls as incomes rise,' at http://www.guardian. co.uk/uk/2010/nov/15/money-happy-europe-wellbeing-income

3. BBC News (2009), 'Depression looms as global crisis', at http://news.bbc.co.uk/1/hi/8230549.stm

4. E Halliwell (2010), *Mindfulness Report* (Mental Health Foundation)

5. Techradar.com (2008), 'Is humanity drowning in a
    sea of gadgets?', at http://www.techradar.com/news/
    world-of-tech/is-humanity-drowning-in-a-sea-of-
    gadgets--270462

6. I Sample (2010), 'Oxford scientist calls for research on
    technology "mind change"', at http://www.guardian.
    co.uk/science/2010/sep/14/oxford-scientist-brain-
    change

7. Cited at Depression in Primary Care, http://www.
    depression-primarycare.co.uk/where.htm

8. Ibid.

9. E Halliwell (2010), *Mindfulness Report* (Mental Health
    Foundation)

10. National Center for Complementary and Alternative
    Medicine, Meditation for Health Purposes, at http://
    www.scribd.com/doc/2175081/Practice-Meditation-
    wwwsanderscontactscom

11. For an extensive database of research papers on
    mindfulness, visit the excellent Mindfulness Research
    Guide at http://www.mindfulexperience.org/. For some
    recent reviews of the evidence, see TS Mars & H Abbey
    (2010), 'Mindfulness meditation practice as a health
    care intervention: A systematic review', *International
    Journal of Osteopathic Medicine* 13(2): 56–66; E
    Halliwell (2010), *Mindfulness Report* (Mental Health
    Foundation); J Greeson (2009), Mindfulness Research

Update: 2008 *Complementary Health Practice Review* 14(1): 110–18; DS Ludwig and J Kabat-Zinn (2008), 'Mindfulness in medicine', *Journal of the American Medical Association* 300(11): 1350–1352; KW Brown *et al.* (2007), 'Mindfulness: Theoretical foundations and evidence for its salutary effects' *Psychological Inquiry* 18(4): 211–237

12. F Zeidan (2010), 'Mindfulness meditation improves cognition: Evidence of brief mental training', *Consciousness and Cognition* 19(2): 597–605, and YY Tang *et al.* (2007), 'Short-term meditation training improves attention and self-regulation', *Proceedings of the National Academy of Sciences* 104(43): 17152–17156

13. E Halliwell (2010), *Mindfulness Report* (Mental Health Foundation)

14. D Black (2010), *Mindfulness Research Monthly* vol. 5, at http://www.mindfulexperience.org/resources/files/MRM_V1N5_june.pdf

CHAPTER 2

1. Thanks to Jonathan Rowson at the RSA for some of these quotes, via his excellent blog post 'Doing and Being' at http://www.rsablogs.org.uk/2010/socialbrain/mindfulness3/

2. American Society of Plastic Surgeons, Report of the 2010 Plastic Surgery Statistics, at http://www.plasticsurgery.org/Documents/news – resources/

statistics/2010–statistics/Top–Level/2010–US–
cosmetic–reconstructive–plastic–surgery–minimally–
invasive–statistics2.pdf

3. Note that the English word 'mindfulness' is often used
    to refer both to the more focused kind of attention
    implied by right concentration and the wider kind of
    awareness implied by right mindfulness.

4. For a full translated text of the Four Foundations of
    Mindfulness, see, for example, http://www.buddhanet.
    net/imol/foudatn.htm

5. William James (1890), *The Principles of Psychology*
    (Holt): 401

6. Sigmund Freud quoted in J Austin (1999), *Selfless
    Insight: Zen and the Meditative Transformations of
    Consciousness* (MIT Press): 79

7. For more on Albert Ellis, visit the Albert Ellis Institute
    at http://www.rebt.org/

8. This is from the opening lines of the Dhammapada:
    'We are what we think/All that we are arises with
    our thoughts/With our thoughts we make the world/
    Speak or act with an impure mind/And trouble will
    follow you/As the wheel follows the ox that draws the
    cart/We are what we think/All that we are arises with
    our thoughts/With our thoughts we make the world'
    quoted at http://www.thebigview.com/buddhism/
    dhammapada–01.html

CHAPTER 3

1. A Bechera *et al.* (1997), 'Deciding Advantageously Before Knowing the Advantageous Strategy', *Science* 275(5304): 1293–1295

2. *Pulse* (2003), 'Explaining the Unexplained to Patients', at http://www.pulsetoday.co.uk/article-content/-/article_display_list/10876393/

3. See, for example, 'MIND on Pain: When Pain Lingers', *Scientific American Mind*, September 2009, at http://www.scientificamerican.com/article.cfm?id=when-pain-lingers

4. Rethink, Physical Health, at http://www.rethink.org/living_with_mental_illness/everyday_living/physical_health_and_wellbeing/staying_healthy/index.html

5. Institute of Heartmath, Science of the Heart: Exploring the Role of the Heart in Human Performance, at http://www.heartmath.org/research/science – of – the – heart/introduction.html

6. J Austin (2009), *Selfless Insight: Zen and the Meditative Transformations of Consciousness* (MIT Press): 8

7. D Cioffi and J Holloway (1993), 'Delayed costs of suppressed pain', *Journal of Personality and Social Psychology* 64: 274–82

8. Thanks to Susan Smalley and Diana Winston for the inspiration for this practice. We highly recommend their book *Fully Present: The Science, Art and Practice of Mindfulness* (2010, Da Capo)

9. B Roth and T Creaser (1997), 'Mindfulness meditation-based stress reduction: experience with a bilingual inner-city program', *Nurse Practitioner* 5: 215

10. J Kabat-Zinn *et al.* (1992), 'Effectiveness of a meditation-based stress reduction program in the treatment of anxiety disorders', *American Journal of Psychiatry* 149: 936–43

11. J Kabat-Zinn *et al.* (1985), 'The clinical use of mindfulness meditation for the self-regulation of chronic pain', *Journal of Behavioural Medicine* 8(2)

12. For those interested in exploring some of these studies in detail, we can recommend the mindfulness research guide website www.mindfulexperience.org. For some reviews and analysis of the evidence, see the following: RA Baer (2003), 'Mindfulness training as a clinical intervention: a conceptual and empirical review', *Clinical Psychology Science and Practice* 10, 125–143; KW Brown *et al.* (2007), 'Mindfulness: Theoretical foundations and evidence for its salutary effects', *Psychological Inquiry* 18: 4, 211–237; J Greeson (2009), Mindfulness research update: 2008 *Complementary Health Practice Review* 14(1): 10–18; P Grossman *et al.* (2004), 'Mindfulness-based stress reduction and health

benefits: A meta-analysis', *Journal of Psychosomatic Research* 57(1), 35–43; E Halliwell (2010), *Mindfulness Report* (Mental Health Foundation); DS Ludwig and J Kabat-Zinn (2008), 'Mindfulness in medicine', *Journal of the American Medical Association* 300(11): 1350–1352; TS Mars and H Abbey (2010), 'Mindfulness meditation practice as a healthcare intervention: A systematic review', *International Journal of Osteopathic Medicine* 13(2): 56–66; M Merkes (2010), 'Mindfulness-based stress reduction for people with chronic diseases', *Australian Journal of Primary Health* 16(3): 200–210; E Bohlmeijer *et al.* (2010), 'The effects of mindfulness-based stress reduction therapy on mental health of adults with a chronic medical disease: A meta-analysis', *Journal of Psychosomatic Research* 68(6): 539–544; and A Chiesa and A Seretti (2011), 'Mindfulness-based interventions for chronic pain: a systematic review of the evidence', *Journal of Complementary Medicine* 17(1): 83–93

13. J Kabat-Zinn (1982), 'An outpatient program in behavioural medicine for chronic pain patients based on the practice of Mindfulness meditation: theoretical considerations and preliminary results', *General Hospital Psychiatry* 4(1): 334

14. J Kabat-Zinn *et al.* (1986), 'Four-year follow-up of a meditation-based program for the self-regulation of chronic pain: Treatment outcomes and compliance', *Clinical Journal of Pain* 2:159–173

15. M Oz (2010), 'Use your brain to relieve pain,' at http://washingtonexaminer.com/entertainment/health/dr-oz-use-your-brain-relieve-pain

16. Fox News (2010), 'To Reduce Pain (and Alter Your Brain), Try Meditation', at http://www.foxnews.com/health/2010/11/18/reduce-pain-alter-brain-try-meditation/

17. E Sternberg (2009), *Healing Spaces: The Science of Place and Wellbeing* (Harvard University Press): 111–14

18. J Kabat-Zinn *et al.* (1998), 'Influence of a mindfulness meditation-based stress reduction intervention on rates of skin clearing in patients with moderate to severe psoriasis undergoing phototherapy (UVB) and photochemotherapy (PUVA)', *Psychosomatic Medicine* 60(5): 625–32

19. R J Davidson *et al.* (2003), 'Alterations in brain and immune function produced by mindfulness meditation', *Psychosomatic Medicine* 65: 564–70

20. L Witek-Janusek (2008), 'Effect of mindfulness-based stress reduction on immune function, quality of life and coping in women newly diagnosed with early stage breast cancer', *Brain, Behaviour and Immunity* 22(6): 968–81

21. J Greeson (2009), Mindfulness Research Update: 2008, *Complementary Health Practice Review* 14(1): 10–18

22. J D Creswell *et al.* (2009), 'Mindfulness meditation training effects on CD4+ T lymphocytes in HIV-1 infected adults: A small randomized controlled trial', *Brain, Behaviour and Immunity* 23(2): 184–88

23. P Robinson *et al.* (2003), 'Psycho-endocrine-immune response to mindfulness-based stress reduction in individuals infected with the human immunodeficiency virus: a quasiexperimental study', *Journal Alternative Complementary Medicine* 9(5): 683–94

24. E Epel *et al.* (2004), 'Accelerated telomere shortening in response to life stress', *Proceedings of the National Academy of Sciences* 101(49): 17312–15

25. *Science Daily* (2010), 'Positive Wellbeing to Higher Telomerase: Psychological Changes from Meditation Training Linked to Cellular Health', at http://www.sciencedaily.com/releases/2010/11/101103171642.htm

26. See, for example, BBC News (2004), 'Stress "may speed up cell ageing"' at http://news.bbc.co.uk/1/hi/4054207.stm

27. See R A Baer (2003), 'Mindfulness training as a clinical intervention: a conceptual and empirical review', *Clinical Psychology Science & Practice* 10: 125–43

CHAPTER 4

1. BBC News (2009), 'Depression looms as global crisis', at http://news.bbc.co.uk/1/hi/8230549.stm

2. D Kessler *et al.* (2005), 'Lifetime prevalence and age-of-onset distributions of DSM-IV disorders in the National Comorbidity Survey Replication', *Archives of General Psychiatry* 62(6): 593–602

3. BBC News (2009), 'Depression looms as global crisis', at http://news.bbc.co.uk/1/hi/8230549.stm

4. See Mental Health Foundation (2007), *The Fundamental Facts: The Latest Facts and Figures on Mental Health* (London: Mental Health Foundation)

5. For example, see 'Does Depression Shrink Your Brain?', at http://abcnews.go.com/Health/Depression/story?id=3885728&page=2

6. See M Williams *et al.* (2007), *The Mindful Way Through Depression: Freeing Yourself From Chronic Unhappiness* (Guilford): 16–17

7. See Mental Health Foundation (2007), *The Fundamental Facts: The Latest Facts and Figures on Mental Health* (London: Mental Health Foundation)

8. JD Teasdale *et al.* (2000), 'Prevention of relapse/recurrence in major depression by mindfulness-based cognitive therapy', *Journal of Consulting and Clinical Psychology* 68: 615–23

9. SH Ma and JD Teasdale (2004), 'Mindfulness-based cognitive therapy for depression: replication and exploration of differential relapse prevention effects', *Journal of Consulting and Clinical Psychology* 72: 31–40

10. W Kuyken *et al.* (2008), 'Mindfulness-based cognitive therapy to prevent relapse in recurrent depression', *Journal of Consulting and Clinical Psychology* 76(6): 966–78

11. Mindful.org (2010), 'Treating depression: medication or meditation', at http://mindful.org/news/treating-depression-medication-or-meditation

12. See T Barnhofer *et al.* (2009), 'Mindfulness-based cognitive therapy as a treatment for chronic depression: a preliminary study', *Behaviour Research and Therapy* 47(5): 366–73; M Kenny and JMG Williams (2007), 'Treatment-resistant depressed patients show a good response to mindfulness-based cognitive therapy', *Behaviour Research and Therapy* 45(3): 617–25; SJ Eisendrath *et al.* (2008), 'Mindfulness-based cognitive therapy for treatment-resistant depression: a pilot study', *Psychotherapy & Psychosomatics* 77: 319–20

13. J Kabat-Zinn *et al.* (1992), 'Effectiveness of a meditation-based stress reduction program in the treatment of anxiety disorders', *American Journal of Psychiatry* 149: 936–43

14. SG Hofmann *et al.* (2010), 'The effect of mindfulness-based therapy on anxiety and depression: A meta-analytic review', *Journal of Consulting and Clinical Psychology* 78(2): 169-83. Reported at http://www.scientificmindfulness.com/2010/05/effects-of-mindfulness-based-therapy-on.html

15. See S Smalley and D Winston (2010), *Fully Present: The Science, Art and Practice of Mindfulness* (Da Capo): 105

16. See Scientific Mindfulness, 'Mindfulness Meditation as a Potential Treatment for ADHD,' at http://www.scientificmindfulness.com/2010/04/mindfulness-meditation-as-potential.html

17. See 'Challenging GAD with Mindfulness' at http://psychescientia.blogspot.com/2008/05/challenging-gad-with-mindfulness.html

18. Action For Happiness, 'Why Happiness Matters,' at http://www.actionforhappiness.org/why-happiness-matters/

19. M Klatt *et al.* (2009), 'Effects of low-dose mindfulness-based stress reduction (MBSR-ld) on working adults', *Health Education and Behaviour* 36(3): 601–614

20. JD Teasdale *et al.* (2002), 'Metacognitive awareness and prevention of relapse in depression: Empirical evidence', *Journal of Consulting and Clinical Psychology* 70(2): 275–87

21. S Jain *et al.* (2007), 'A randomized controlled trial of mindfulness meditation versus relaxation training: effects on distress, positive states of mind, rumination, and distraction', *Annals of Behavioural Medicine* 33(1): 11–21

22. See BBC News (2010), 'People spend "half their waking hours daydreaming"', at http://www.bbc.co.uk/news/health-11741350

23. W Kuyken *et al.* (2010), 'How does mindfulness-based cognitive therapy work?', *Behaviour Research and Therapy* 48(11): 1105–1112

24. See KW Brown *et al.* (2007), 'Mindfulness: Theoretical foundations and evidence for its salutary effects', *Psychological Inquiry* 18(4): 211-37; and J Greeson (2009), Mindfulness Research Update: 2008 *Complementary Health Practice Review* 14(1): 110–18

25. Ibid.

26. See Chögyam Trungpa, 'The Education of the Warrior', available at http://www.poetry-chaikhana.com/T/TrungpaChogy/EducationofW.htm

27. For more on this, see S Begley (2007), *Train Your Mind, Change Your Brain: How a New Science Reveals Our Extraordinary Potential to Transform Ourselves* (Ballantine)

28. See, for example, D Kahneman *et al.* (2004) 'Toward national wellbeing accounts', at http://www.krueger.princeton.edu/Toward%20Wellbeing.pdf

29. EA Maguire *et al.* (2000), 'Navigation-related structural change in the hippocampi of taxi drivers', *Proceedings of the National Academy of Sciences* 97(8): 4398–4403

30. See, for example, BBC News (2004), 'Learning Languages "boosts brain"', at http://news.bbc.co.uk/1/hi/health/3739690.stm

31. B Johannson (2006), 'Music and brain plasticity', *European Review* 14(1): 49–64

32. For more on the work of Professor Davidson, see the laboratory's website at http://psyphz.psych.wisc.edu/

33. For more, see D Goleman (2003), 'Finding happiness: Cajole your brain to lean to the left', *New York Times*, at http://www.nytimes.com/2003/02/04/health/behaviour-finding-happiness-cajole-your-brain-to-lean-to-the-left.html?pagewanted=1; also, RJ Davidson and W Irwin (1999), 'The functional neuroanatomy of emotion and affective style', *Trends in Cognitive Sciences* 3(1): 11–21

34. RJ Davidson *et al.* (2003), 'Alterations in brain and immune function produced by mindfulness meditation', *Psychosomatic Medicine* 65: 564–70

35. S Lazar *et al.* (2005), 'Meditation experience is associated with increased cortical thickness', *Neuroreport* 16(17): 1893–97

36. *Science Daily* (2011), 'Mindfulness Meditation Training Changes Brain Structure in Eight Weeks,' at http://www.sciencedaily.com/releases/2011/01/110121144007.htm, based on the original paper, B Hölzel *et al.* (2011), 'Mindfulness practice leads to increases in regional brain gray matter density', *Psychiatry Research: Neuroimaging* 191(1): 36

CHAPTER 5

1. J Bradshaw (1996) *Bradshaw on the Family: A New Way of Creating Solid Self-Esteem* (Health Communications): 108

2. See, for example, http://www.drugscope.org.uk/ resources/drugsearch/drugsearchpages/tobacco

3. See BBC News (2005), 'How much is too much?', at http://news.bbc.co.uk/1/hi/magazine/4188071.stm

4. Reuters (2008), 'More Americans than ever are obese', at http://www.reuters.com/article/2009/07/08/us-obesity-usa-idUSTRE5674UF20090708

5. P Chodron (2005), *When Things Fall Apart: Heart Advice for Difficult Times* (Element): 15

6. See, for example, National Institute on Drug Abuse, 'Anxiety and stress found to promote cocaine use in rats', at http://archives.drugabuse.gov/NIDA_Notes/ NNVol11N4/Anxiety.html

7. C Trungpa (revised edn; 1996), *The Sacred Path of the Warrior* (Shambhala): see Chapter 7, 'The Cocoon'

8. BK Hölzel *et al.* (2010), 'Stress reduction correlates with structural changes in the amygdala', *Social Cognitive and Affective Neuroscience* 5(1): 11–17

9. JC Cresswell *et al.* (2007), 'Neural correlates of dispositional mindfulness during affect labeling', *Psychosomatic Medicine* 69(6): 560–65

10. E Luders *et al.* (2009), 'The underlying anatomical correlates of long-term meditation: Larger hippocampal and frontal volumes of gray matter', *NeuroImage* 45(3): 672–78

11. LC Chu (2010), 'The benefits of meditation vis-à-vis emotional intelligence, perceived stress and negative mental health', *Stress and Health* 26: 169–80

12. See for example, B Kilm *et al.* (2010), 'Effectiveness of a mindfulness-based cognitive therapy program as an adjunct to pharmacotherapy in patients with panic disorder', *Journal of Anxiety Disorders* 24(6): 590–95; and S Evans *et al.* (2008), 'Mindfulness-based cognitive therapy for generalized anxiety disorder', *Journal of Anxiety Disorders* 22(4): 716–21

13. See KW Brown *et al.* (2007), 'Mindfulness: theoretical foundations and evidence for its salutary effects', *Psychological Inquiry* 18(4): 211–37; and SS Welch *et al.* (2006), 'Mindfulness in dialectical behaviour therapy (DBT) for borderline personality disorder', in RA Baer (ed) (2005), *Mindfulness-based treatment approaches: clinician's guide to evidence base and applications* (Academic Press): 117–38

14. NN Singh *et al.* (2007), 'Adolescents with conduct disorder can be mindful of their aggressive behaviour', *Journal of Emotional and Behavioural Disorders*: 56–63; M Samuelson *et al.* (2007), 'Mindfulness-based stress reduction in Massachusetts correctional facilities', *The*

Prison Journal 87(2): 254–58; and S Bogels *et al.* (2008), 'Mindfulness training for adolescents with externalizing disorders and their parents', *Behavioural and Cognitive Psychotherapy*:193–209

15. WL Heppner *et al.* (2008), 'Mindfulness as a means of reducing aggressive behaviour: Dispositional and situational evidence', *Aggressive Behaviour*: 486–96; and KW Brown *et al.* (2007), 'Mindfulness: theoretical foundations and evidence for its salutary effects', *Psychological Inquiry* 18(4): 211–37

16. GA Marlatt *et al.* (1984), 'Effects of meditation and relaxation training upon alcohol misuse in male social drinkers', in DH Shapiro and RN Walsh (eds) (1984), *Meditation: Classic and contemporary perspectives* (Aldine)

17. S Bowen *et al.* (2009), 'Mindfulness-based relapse prevention for substance use disorders: A pilot efficacy trial', *Substance Abuse* 30(4): 295–305

18. JM Davis (2007), 'A pilot study on mindfulness-based stress reduction for smokers', *BMC Complementary and Alternative Medicine* 7: 2

19. JL Kristeller *et al.* (2006), 'Mindfulness-based approaches to eating disorders', in RA Baer (ed) (2005), *Mindfulness-based treatment approaches: clinician's guide to evidence base and applications* (Academic Press): 75–93

20. Reported at http://weightloss.about.com/b/2011/01/26/ mindfulness-matters.htm and http://www. huffingtonpost.com/wray-herbert/meditation-research_b_780525.html

21. D Gilbert and J Waltz (2010), 'Mindfulness and Health Behaviours', *Mindfulness* 1: 227–34

22. K Brown, T Kasser *et al.* (2009), 'When what one has is enough: Mindfulness, financial desire discrepancy, and subjective wellbeing', *Journal of Research in Personality*, at http://www.psych.rochester.edu/SDT/ documents/2009_BrownKasserRyanLinleyOrzech_ JRP.pdf

CHAPTER 6

1. AP Jha *et al.* (2007), 'Mindfulness training modifies subsystems of attention', *Cognitive, Affective & Behavioural Neuroscience* 7: 109–19

2. HA Slagter *et al.* (2007), 'Mental Training Affects Distribution of Limited Brain Resources', *PLoS Biology* 5(6): e138

3. LT Cullen (2006), 'How to get smarter, one breath at a time: scientists find that meditation not only reduces stress but also reshapes the brain', *Time*, at http://www. time.com/time/magazine/article/0,9171,1147167,00.html

4. E Luders *et al.* (2009), 'The underlying anatomical correlates of long-term meditation: Larger hippocampal

and frontal volumes of gray matter', *NeuroImage* 45(3): 672–78

5. For more on emotional contagion, see D Hamilton (2011), *The Contagious Power of Thinking: How your thoughts can influence the world* (Hay House)

6. For more on work-related stress, see http://www.cipd. co.uk/subjects/health/stress/stress.htm and http://www. healthyworkinglives.com/advice/work-relatedillness- injury/stress-workplace.aspx; Health and Safety Executive (2004). 'Helping business cut the cost of work-related stress', available at http://www.hse.gov.uk/ press/2004/c04046.htm

7. For a full description of Transport for London's use of mindfulness for their employees, see the case study in E Halliwell (2010), *Mindfulness Report* (Mental Health Foundation): 70

8. See http://www.cipd.co.uk/subjects/health/stress/stress. htm

9. INSEAD (2007), 'Understanding and responding to societal demands on corporate responsibility (response)'. Final report available at http://www.insead. edu/v1/ibis/response_project/documents/Response_ FinalReport.pdf

10. PE Flaxman and FW Bond (2006), 'Acceptance and commitment therapy in the workplace', in RA Baer (ed) (2005), *Mindfulness-based treatment approaches:*

clinician's guide to evidence base and applications (Academic Press): 377–82

11. U Kirk *et al.* (2011), 'Interoception drives increased rational decision-making in meditators playing the ultimatum game', *Frontiers In Neuroscience* 18(5): 49

12. MS Krasner *et al.* (2009), 'Association of an educational program in mindful communication with burnout, empathy, and attitudes among primary care physicians', *Journal of the American Medical Association* 302 (12): 1284–93

13. SL Shapiro *et al.* (1998), 'Effects of Mindfulness-based stress reduction on medical and premedical students', *Journal of Behavioural Medicine* 21: 581–99

14. L Grepmair *et al.* (2007), 'Promotion of mindfulness in psychotherapists in training influences the treatment results of their patients: A randomized, double-blind, controlled study', *Psychotherapy and Psychosomatics* 76(6)

15. RJ Semple *et al.* (2006), 'Mindfulness-based cognitive therapy for children', in RA Baer (ed) (2005), *Mindfulness-based treatment approaches: clinician's guide to evidence base and applications* (Academic Press): 143–65

16. See http://www.thehawnfoundation.org/mindup-studies

17. See O Bowcott (2009), 'Tories slam doctors for drugging children', The Guardian, at http://www.guardian.co.uk/society/2009/oct/30/conservatives-nhs-children-drugs-mental-health

18. CA Burke (2009), 'Mindfulness-based approaches with children and adolescents: A preliminary review of current research in an emergent field', *Journal of Child and Family Studies*, available at http://www.springerlink.com/content/e1638088141n327m/

19. C Vieten and J Astin (2008), 'Effects of a mindfulness-based intervention during pregnancy on prenatal stress and mood: results of a pilot study', *Archives of Women's Mental Health* 1(1): 67–74

20. See K Brown *et al.* (2007), 'Mindfulness: theoretical foundations and evidence for its salutary effects', *Psychological Inquiry* 18(4): 211–37; D Siegel (2007), *The Mindful Brain: Reflection and Attunement in the Cultivation of Wellbeing* (WW Norton); J Williams (2008), 'Mindfulness, depression and modes of mind', *Cognitive Therapy and Research* 32(6): 721–33; PA Frewen *et al.* (2008), 'Letting go: Mindfulness and negative automatic thinking', *Cognitive Therapy and Research* 32(6): 758–74; WL Heppner and MH Kernis (2007), 'Quiet ego functioning: the complementary roles of mindfulness, authenticity, and secure high self-esteem', *Psychological Inquiry* 18(4): 248–51; PR Shaver *et al.* (2007), 'Social foundations of the capacity for mindfulness: an attachment perspective', *Psychological Inquiry* 18(4): 264–71

21. D Siegel (2007), *The Mindful Brain: Reflection and Attunement in the Cultivation of Wellbeing* (WW Norton)

22. JW Carson *et al.* (2006), 'Mindfulness-based relationship enhancement (MBRE) in couples', in RA Baer (ed) (2005), *Mindfulness-based treatment approaches: clinician's guide to evidence base and applications* (Academic Press) 309–29

23. From World Wildlife Fund (2010), 'Common Cause: The Case for Working with Our Cultural Values', quoting KW Brown and T Kasser (2005), 'Are psychological and ecological wellbeing compatible? The role of values, mindfulness and lifestyle', *Social Indicators Research* 74: 349–68

CHAPTER 7

1. N Farb *et al.* (2007), 'Attending to the present: mindfulness meditation reveals distinct neural modes of self-reference', *Social Cognitive and Affective Neuroscience* 2(4): 313–22. For a good summary and explanation of this paper's findings, see D Rock (2009), 'The neuroscience of mindfulness', *Psychology Today*, at www.psychologytoday.com/blog/your-brain-work/200910/the-neuroscience-mindfulness

ACKNOWLEDGEMENTS

The contents of this book have been inspired by both
ancient wisdom and modern research. It is only thanks
to the patience and generosity of many people over
thousands of years that we have access to teachings on
mindfulness and meditation. Lineages of wise practitioners
have generously passed down these teachings through the
centuries, while the recent attention of scientists has given
mindfulness a secular credibility that has enabled many
more people to access its benefits. We would like to thank
you all.

We would especially like to thank those people who have
generously given their knowledge and time during the
preparation of this book – people such as Mark Williams,
Sara Lazar, Alan Wallace, Paramabandhu Groves and
Michael Chaskalson. Also invaluable have been our 'case
studies', who've allowed us to share their experience of
mindfulness practice – we hope their stories are as inspiring
to you as they are to us. Our admiration and gratitude go to
Jon Kabat-Zinn for his seminal work in creating, teaching,

researching and nurturing mindfulness-based stress reduction, and to all those who are continuing the work of finding ever more skilful means for bringing mindfulness to the world.

We have both been extremely fortunate to encounter the teachings of Chögyam Trungpa Rinpoche and Sakyong Mipham Rinpoche, along with many other authentic teachers in the Shambhala Buddhist tradition, whose wisdom and generosity have offered us a path of inquiry along which we continue to stumble.

Thanks also to the fabulous team at Hay House UK, who responded so favourably to our idea for this book and helped steer it through to publication. We'd especially like to thank our editor, Carolyn Thorne, who has been an unflappable and encouraging presence whenever we started to flap or get disheartened, our copy-editor Barbara Vesey for refining our words, Jessica Crocket, Jo Burgess, Jo Lal and Nicola Fletcher for all their efforts to promote the book, publisher Michelle Pilley for her belief in it, and editorial assistant Amy Kiberd for her excellent support. We'd also like to thank all the staff at Hay House in the US, who worked with us on the second edition of *The Mindful Manifesto* – in particular Patty Gift, for her enthusiasm for and commitment to publishing it for American readers, and Sally Mason for her careful work on the manuscript.

Ed: I'm profoundly grateful to all those who have helped me on my ongoing mindfulness journey – there are many more of you than I have room to mention here. My main meditation instructors Tom Dillon, Yves Bret and Caroline

Helm have been patient, fearless, kind and endlessly encouraging – heartfelt thanks to all of you. I'd also like to thank all those who live, work and practise at the Dechen Chöling retreat centre in France, where I spent a year deepening my meditation practice in 2006. Thanks also to everyone at the London Shambhala Meditation Centre, who offered a place of refuge and inspiration for me at a time when I was desperately searching for it.

Gratitude and love go to my parents, Jill and Ivor Halliwell, who were instrumental in nurturing my early spiritual life and have always given their non-judgemental support, despite all the mistakes I have made over the years. Thanks and love also go to Rex Bradley, who offered frequent wise guidance in recent times, along with a steady, kind and gentle presence that taught me much about mindfulness. My brothers Nick, Julian and Jeremy, and close friends James Lowen and Will Fuller, have also given me much-appreciated support over the years, in both joyful and difficult times.

Thanks to Steph Ebdon, my agent, who has offered, and continues to offer, much good advice on the planning and development of this book. Thanks as well go to everyone at the Mental Health Foundation for responding so positively to the suggestion of a research report on mindfulness, and kindly allowing me to reproduce some of the case studies used in that report here – and thanks to Dylan Schlosberg for making that project possible. Appreciation also goes to David Shariatmadari and Andrew Brown for allowing me to write about meditation and Buddhism for *The Guardian*, expanding my journalistic career into the areas I care most about.

I'm also grateful to everyone who has helped me begin to develop as a mindfulness teacher – to Cindy Cooper, Karunavira, Rebecca Crane, Pamela Erdmann, Jody Mardula, Michael Chaskalson and all the other expert trainers and staff at the Bangor University Centre for Mindfulness Research and Practice, to Tessa Watt and Debbie Johnson at Being Mindful for showing the way and encouraging me to teach with them, and to Morgwn Rimel, Caroline Brimmer and colleagues at the School of Life for offering me another space in which to teach. Special thanks to everyone in Shambhala for the years of insight, training and support on the path, without whom all this simply wouldn't work. And of course, thanks to everyone who has participated in any of the courses I have led or assisted on – your dedication, openness and willingness to practise continue to inspire and teach me.

Finally, I'd like to thank my wonderful wife Victoria, for managing the miraculously mindful feat of putting up with and encouraging me during the writing process (not just once, but twice, the second time while pregnant!), as well as for having the inspiration, courage and persistence to set up Mindfulness Sussex, and generally for being the most amazing, beautiful, grounded, loving person I could ever have hoped for as a partner. Huge love and gratitude also to our son Arthur, who is already a master at bringing me back to attention, as well as enriching our lives in ways I could only have imagined before. My share of this book is dedicated from my heart to theirs.

Jonty: I'm indebted to all those who have encouraged
and taught me over the last 38 years. Their generosity
and kindness has allowed me not only to gain from their
understanding and insight but also to grow in confidence
in my own inherent wisdom, so that I have been able
to believe that I have something interesting to say! In
particular I want to thank those people who have, without
criticism, pushed me to 'raise my gaze' and broaden my
horizon, letting me glimpse what words like helping, caring
and healing really mean – beyond the narrow confines
of a purely biological model of health and illness. While
at medical school I was fortunate enough to meet Eric
Shepherd and Simon Read, who are really responsible
for starting off this process of exploration. Then, as I
embarked on my training to become a family doctor, I had
the example of those such as David Poole, Roger Higgs,
Annalee Curran and Tina Buchannan – all of whom
continue to inspire me to be the best doctor that I can be.

I am indebted to Jim O'Neill and Peter Conradi, whose love
and guidance have transformed the lives of a great many of
the people they have taught, mine being just one of them.
And to Julien Diaz for reminding me to take care of my
body occasionally as well!

I also owe a huge debt of gratitude to my partners and all
the staff at Manor Place Surgery. They know what it is to
care, genuinely and deeply, for the patients they look after.
I feel lucky to be a part of the team, and I thank them for
the stability and support they offer me. It is this that has
allowed me to branch out in so many different directions
over recent years in the sure knowledge that if, and when,

I lose sight of what is important they will be there to bring what really matters back into focus. And, of course, equally important in this process are the many patients who have worked, and continue to work, alongside me in taking care of their hearts, minds and bodies, and from whom I have learned so much. Helping is always a two-way street, and the generosity of my patients in sharing their pain is a gift, not a burden, and one that gives me inspiration and sustenance without which my life would be all the poorer.

My share of this book would not have been possible without the love and support of my friends and family who have been so accepting of my constant preoccupation with writing it, and have come to know better than most that theory does not always translate into practice when it comes to being mindful! Although their contribution to the process does, of course, go much deeper than simply that of kindly onlookers. I am sure I am not unique in wanting to thank my parents, Frank and Rosemary, for all their love and support throughout my life, but the sacrifices that they have made so that I could have the opportunities I have had are truly humbling and a great inspiration to me.

And finally, love and thanks to my partner Tye who, despite being thousands of miles away for a lot of the time I have been writing this book, has spent many hours engaged in long transatlantic phone calls calming and encouraging me and, without whom, my world would be a much less inspiring place.

INDEX

This index is in word-by-word alphabetical order.

ABOUT THE AUTHORS

 **Dr Jonty Heaversedge** is a GP in a large practice in southeast London. He completed a degree in psychology and then a Master's in Mental Health Studies, and continues to pursue a particular interest in the psychological health and wellbeing of his patients. Jonty is a regular contributor to television and radio, and has become an increasingly familiar face on the BBC. Visit his website: http://www.drjonty.com/

 **Ed Halliwell** is a UK-based mindfulness teacher and writer. He leads mindfulness courses and retreats in London, Sussex and across the south east of England, working with a wide range of individuals, groups and organizations. He is the author of the Mental Health Foundation's 'Be Mindful' report and writes for *The Guardian* newspaper on meditation and wellbeing. He also writes a regular blog for mindful.org, and is a faculty member at the School of Life in London. Visit him at http://edhalliwell.com/

THE MINDFUL MANIFESTO ONLINE

WWW.THEMINDFULMANIFESTO.COM

Support the Mindful Manifesto by visiting our website, where you'll find:

- all the latest mindfulness news, including details of our talks, courses, coaching and workshops

- audio versions of exercises from *The Mindful Manifesto*, to help you get started in your practice

- discussion of the latest developments in mindfulness, via the Mindful Manifesto blog

- details of how to sign up for our newsletter and contact us about our work.